Sarada Ramakrishna Vivekananda Associations
of Oregon, San Francisco,
& Hawaii

Reclaiming Kundalini Yoga

by
Babaji Bob Kindler

Published by SRV Associations
P.O. Box 1364
Honoka'a, Hawaii 96727
email: srvinfo@srv.org
website: www.srv.org

The publication of this book was made possible by donations
from friends and students of SRV Associations.

Printed in the United States of America
ISBN 978-1-891893-11-7

Acknowledgements

Our thanks to Ramnand Tiwari of Pilgrim's Books for the use of many of the
images in this book, including the cover image of Lord Siva.

Our gratitude is extended to the Ramakrishna-Vivekananda Center of New York
for permission to print the poem on pgs. 55-57, taken from the Gospel of Sri
Ramakrishna, pgs, 261-262, Copyright 1942, by Swami Nikhilananda.

Our gratitude is extended to Swami Vijnananandaji, direct disciple of Sri
Ramakrishna, for his English translation of the Srimad Devi Bhagavatam,
Munshiram Manoharlal edition, from which I have selected several short sec-
tions for retranslation.

Contents

List of Illustrations/Charts

Dedication

She who, since birth, has ever led me on

Through paths of trouble to perfection's

goal,

Mother-wise, in Her own sweet and playful

ways,

She, who has always through my life

inspired My understanding,

She my Mother, She, The ALL,

is my resort,

whether my work O'erflow with full

fruition,

or with none.

Swami Vivekananda
– From the poem,
"Hymns to the Goddess"

Introduction

The ancient and rather obscure system of *Kundalini Yoga*, though quite esoteric by way of practice and principles, has nevertheless reached a wide cross section of living beings in recent times, albeit only on a surface level.   Once held as a deep secret among the spiritually elite and quietly practiced among those willing to undergo specific training with adept preceptors to achieve qualification for spiritual life, this interior Yoga, much like the Eight-limbed Yoga of Patanjali, has suffered greatly at the hands of those who have attempted to turn its noble tenets into a regimen for body postures, breathing exercises, and the study of the human nervous system alone.

Over the past half century certain questionable human factions hiding behind such noble traditions as Tantricism, Shaivism, and Sikhism, have arrived in the West and tried to capitalize upon Kundalini Yoga's intriguing tenets and axioms. And in order to do so, given the materialistic nature of the western peoples, these spurious teachers — always with an eye out for personal monetary gain and attended and followed about by plenty of scandal — gathered Kundalini's most rudimentary teachings and, instead of using them as fundamental starting points, rendered them into the entire scope of its presentation.   The result is that contemporary Kundalini Yoga is now a pale, wan, and spiritually ineffective caricature of itself, brought down and restricted to a mere collection of asanas and breathing exercises, all intended to bring about an increased flow of life force to be utilized for health of the body, pleasure for the senses, and happiness for the mind.

However, the main fact of life and existence, as Lord Buddha and other luminaries have declared, is that suffering is wholly inescapable; it attends human birth and embodiment as flies attend a feast. This fact is non-negotiable, no matter who or what the structure. In short, there is no lasting health on the physical level, nor is there any true happiness in this life. Birth, growth, disease, decay, old age, and death accompany all beings who dare to enter into the world of name and form.

It is for this primary reason that salient spiritual systems left behind by world teachers, with their valuable principles and teachings, are directed towards humanity so that beings may shore themselves up against the many vagaries and vicissitudes of life, which are mostly the effects or repercussions of accrued karma from past lifetimes. To strip these living philosophical bridges of their inherent spiritual power is to do a huge injustice to the great souls who have taken the pains to drive their subtle but massive structural columns deep into the muddy river bed of humanity's individual and collective mind.

And so, the purpose of this small book, replete with a few original teaching charts useful as visual aids, is to reclaim the magnanimous Kundalini Yoga system back from modern presenters who have, deviously or ignorantly, magnified the obvious and omitted the essential in it. To accomplish this task within such a brief condensation and summary, it will be helpful to refer to the origins of Kundalini Yoga so as to be able to draw the teaching principles from them. This alone will reveal it to be of ancient and ultimate nature and character. Thankfully, there is a Vedic source for this great system, called the *Yoga-Kundalini Upanisad*. Wherever the Upanisads (Vedanta) are involved, one can feel fully assured that the authentic, the genuine, the highest and best about Divine Reality is being declared. Within the parameters of such a timeless reference point our study can go forth famously.

And if one adds to this the many mentions of the Kundalini Shakti and Her Tantric system found in the great contemporary work on true spirituality, *The Gospel of Sri Ramakrishna*, which is replete with the Great Master's descriptions of both the philosophy itself and His experiences with it, a more complete rendering of the original fabric and intent of Kundalini Yoga can be re-introduced. In this way we will proceed to unwrap some of the basic and essential tenets of one of the most grand and noble inward-moving vehicles of Mother India's spiritual treasure-house of working philosophy.

In addition to reclaiming the Kundalini philosophy itself, there is a second type of reclamation which this book wants to achieve — that of restoring ownership of our true divine nature into our own hands once again. Called by the name *Atman* in the Vedanta, or *Prajna Param* in Buddhism, the original nature of mankind is not limited to the individual, collective, or even the cosmic level of selfhood, but points to the existence of an underlying, eternal, and all-pervasive Self which is inclusive of these three and transcendent of them as well. It is the untimely loss of memory of this Ultimate Nature, called Pure Consciousness, Timeless Awareness, Buddha Mind, and Original Mind, which must be regained. Dreams, fantasies, projections, fabrications — all of these and more are the products of the mind which has forgotten its immovable and impeccable Nature, which has overlayed or superimposed all manner of presumptions and improbabilities over this otherwise nonvibratory and always stationary and serene Self.

And so the word "reclaiming" takes on two shades of meaning here: one, to strip the Kundalini Yoga system of the many layers and encrustations of contemporary concealment so as to reveal its original tenets once again; and two, to restore it to the powerful and effective pathway to Self-realization that it once was — and still is when utilized by an authentic master and adept practitioner. To these ends the present work at hand turns its rapt attentions.

≈ 1 ≈

"Straightening the Coil"

Beginnings: The Role of Food and Prana in Self-Realization

"Have you straightened your coil yet?" In ancient times and olden days of India this may well have been the surprising question first asked of the sincere aspirant seeking refuge in the rarefied atmosphere of "Holy Company," known as *Sadhu Satsanga* by the revered sages and seers. Short of a positive response, the seeker would be instructed in preliminary practices for initial qualification, and thus ushered into the process of straightening forthwith. This effort of the individual to gain true freedom is called *sadhana* in India, the practice of purificatory techniques designed to engage the aspirant in the quest for purity and enlightenment of mind.

The situation today is not much different than in times of old. That is, there are a multitude of compacted human coils which need to be uncurled and released, their inherent powers brought forth to enliven life and mind. This concentrated power is *Kundalini*, which is more like a living, conscious intelligence *(shaktiman)* than a secondary power *(shakti)*.

The Sanskrit word "*Kunda*" means "coiled up," so the implication is that there is a mighty force, albeit subtle and inward, lying within the regions of the triple human body (physical, subtle, and causal — i.e., *sthula, sukshma,* and *karana*, or, body, mind, and intelligence). Like any good *Yoga*, the purpose of Kundalini Yoga and its practices is to get ahold of this spiritual force and bring it to the fore to effect the highest good at the individual, collective, and cosmic levels (another designation of the three worlds/bodies listed above). To sufficiently illustrate this, an old story, cited by Swami Vivekananda in his book, *Raja Yoga,* can be utilized.

Once, a man was imprisoned in a tall tower by an evil king. The man managed to send a message to his beloved. The message read, *"Come tonight in secret and bring with you a beetle, some honey, a thread, some string, and some rope."* Wondering at this strange list, the woman nevertheless brought the items that night. Then he called down to her, "Tie the thread to the beetle's leg and put some honey on its feelers. Then place the beetle on the tower with its head facing upwards." The beetle, smelling the honey, then went forward to retrieve it, and when it reached the high window of the tower the man plucked it up and grabbed the thread. Then he called down to his friend, "Tie one end of the string to the thread." The man then pulled the string up via the thread. Then he called down, "Now tie the string to the rope." The rest of this story's implications are obvious.

It is in this way that the marvelous spiritual force within the human being is gotten ahold of by using preliminary means. To put it briefly, the spiritual power is brought to bear by securing possession of the refined prana, and this prana, at its different levels, is seized by becoming aware, or sensitive, or conscious, of both the need for refinement of mind and the divine presence or energy which lies at the substratum of all phenomena. Food, what sustains human life, is the gross or outer representation of all this. And here is where Kundalini Yoga and its practices really begin.

Before an explication of food and its role in spiritual life is undertaken, it must be said that living beings operate at many different levels of consciousness. For purposes of simplification, and though there are several subdivisions that can be noted, we can say here that two of these levels are most obvious, namely, as Lord Buddha put it, the awakened and the unawakened. Regarding the former class, "straightening the coil," or awakening the Kundalini Shakti, is not anymore necessary. These adepts can both slough off their bodies in a timely fashion, and return to other forms (if they so choose) — all in higher Consciousness, i.e., knowing that the Soul, Atman, is birthless and deathless.

Recognizing this, we can then take up the latter category of beings, the unawakened, who number in the billions in this present time. It is for these suffering (and enjoying) masses that philosophical systems like Kundalini Yoga, with close associations to religion and spiritual practices, are most helpful. And here we also point to the common denominator of food, that which sustains all. One of the great sayings, or mantras, in India, is, *"anne hidam sarvam prathistam — All here is sustained by food."* Further, other slokas of the scriptures state that everything here on this plane of existence is food for others, meaning that even one's body becomes food for others in the end, like for animals, insects, fire, etc. One is reminded of the case of the lamas living in Tibet who, when nearing the moment of passage from the body, merely instruct that their dead corpses be placed on the top of mountain plateaus so they can serve as food for vultures and other scavengers. They thereby hold both a healthy minimal regard for the expended human body, and a desire for being of use to other beings up until and even after the end of embodied existence.

Realization of the real role of food is at the root of such actions. Primarily, food is not for enjoyment, certainly not for gluttony, or even for health alone. As Sri Krishna states in the *Bhagavad Gita, "Yoga is not for that one who eats too much, or eats too little,"* for in the first scenario one over-stresses the organs and nervous system, and in the other weakens the same. A balanced approach, or a "middle way," is thus prescribed.

The Role of Food & Prana in Self-Realization

"From pure food one gets pure blood. Pure blood produces pure thoughts. Pure thoughts lead to pure mind, and pure mind is Brahman." Sri Sarada Devi

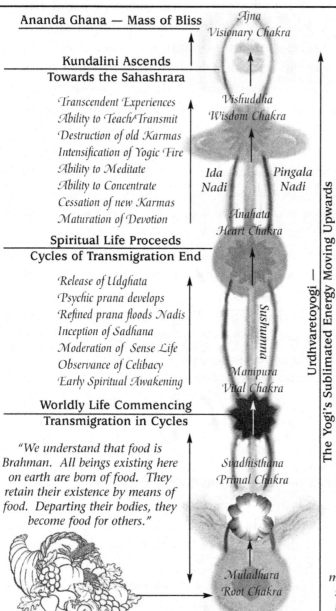

Ananda Ghana — Mass of Bliss

Ajna
Visionary Chakra

Chart by Babaji Bob Kindle
Property of SRV Association

Kundalini Ascends
Towards the Sahashrara

Transcendent Experiences
Ability to Teach/Transmit
Destruction of old Karmas
Intensification of Yogic Fire
Ability to Meditate
Ability to Concentrate
Cessation of new Karmas
Maturation of Devotion

Spiritual Life Proceeds
Cycles of Transmigration End

Release of Udghata
Psychic prana develops
Refined prana floods Nadis
Inception of Sadhana
Moderation of Sense Life
Observance of Celibacy
Early Spiritual Awakening

Worldly Life Commencing
Transmigration in Cycles

"We understand that food is Brahman. All beings existing here on earth are born of food. They retain their existence by means of food. Departing their bodies, they become food for others."

Vishuddha
Wisdom Chakra

Ida Nadi   *Pingala Nadi*

Anahata Heart Chakra

Sushumna

Manipura Vital Chakra

Svadhisthana Primal Chakra

Muladhara Root Chakra

Urdhvaretoyogi — The Yogi's Sublimated Energy Moving Upwards

• *Tejas*

"The emanation that exudes from the pure yogic state is called tejas, a subtle light that transforms. By its presence illumined beings inspire and uplift those who strive and suffer. It also gets utilized for continuing realization and training others. This is spiritual transmission in its fullest manifestation, among those who can inject Brahmajnana and those who have made themselves fit to receive It."

• *Ojas*

"Ojas is the stored up power from pure food and sadhana combined which aids in the release of Kundalini Shakti into higher spiritual centers. Experiences of temporary bliss occur just prior to this but are to be transcended."

• *Mukhya Prana*

"Mukhyaprana supports the organs, sharpens the senses, and maintains life in the body. It must be invigorated by the ingestion of pure food; otherwise, ill health results."

• *Food with Mantra*

"The mantra, uttered in deep meditation, when blessed by such sacred words, renders pure food into prasad." Lord Vasishtha

"anne hidam sarvam prathistham — All is supported by food."

"Food taken with an ignorant or brooding mind turns to poison in the body. Food taken in clarity of mind conduces to perfect health. It is the fire of Yoga in the form of physical, vital, and mental purification that makes the difference." Lord Vasishtha

However, more important to spiritual practice (in all Yogas, really), is the initial and ongoing realization that, as one famous and pithy sloka puts it, "*Food is Brahman.*" And in fact, "*Brahman is the food, Brahman is the offering of the food, Brahman is the one who offers, Brahman is the partaker of the food, Brahman is even the articles upon which the food is placed.*" With this realization in place and foremost in the mind, those who have not yet perceived either their divine inner nature or the purpose for human existence in realizing it, can move towards doing so with all celerity. In other words, and to move directly into the foundational teachings of Kundalini Yoga, food gives us energy. Yet, as Jesus has so cryptically mentioned, "*Man does not live by bread alone.*" Both of these facts imply that there is something potentially and mystically subtle behind the act of eating and, not stopping short of that, around every act which human beings undertake to perform in their lifetimes.

Therefore, in the beginning of this practice the aspirant must become sensitive and start bringing consciousness into everyday life and its activities. And, we must all come to understand that our state of mind while taking food is crucial. As the chart on the facing page teaches, food taken with a depressed, restless, or inadvertent mind turns to poison in the bloodstream, causing discomfort and disease, while food taken while the mind is in a balanced condition turns to nectar, conducing to both perfect health and, more importantly, the possibility of refining the body's energy and turning it in a unique and inward direction. To place a finer point on this, and to introduce an all-important and missing word into the English vocabulary, the presence of *prana*, sometimes called "life-force," presents itself for deeper inspection here.

How to understand prana, then, is the next directive. For a materialistic culture that seldom, if ever, believed in anything which the senses could not perceive, this is going to require a stretch. But a great aid here, as some metaphysicians have noted, is that prana (unlike Spirit) can be inferred.

Somewhat like the presence of unseen fire inferred by the sight of smoke rising off a distant mountain, the movements of the limbs, the "involuntary" operations of some of the body's organs and, especially, the power of the eyes to see and the ears to hear, etc., point unarguably to the presence of a subtle power coursing through the human form. As an advance aside here, this formless form called prana, as it moves inwardly to other internal worlds (as in *"My Father's Mansion has many chambers"*), is Kundalini Shakti; it is one of Her less refined forms which permeate existence at all levels. But more on that soon.

Before we leave the realm of the material, i.e., food and its utilization, the import of "blessing our food" is necessary of explanation. Even if we become conscious of the underlying principles of this practice, the fact remains that access to pure food is difficult for many beings, what to speak of the urge or desire for ingesting organic or untainted foodstuffs. But failing even this, the seers tell us that the power of mantra combined with awakened human consciousness, both brought to bear on food in a conscious way, is a most powerful element in purifying it. To put it in a more comprehendable context, one man may eat rice and vegetables all his life but still remain crude and animalistic, while another man might eat beef and pork and nevertheless develop the mind to a refined level. This all depends upon what we have come to call "blessing our food" in this day and age.

About food blessings in general, and in order to find and utilize those sacred words which will render food pure and edible, a distinction must be made between merely "thanking the Lord" for the presence of food, and the internal awareness which realizes, as has been mentioned already, that food is Brahman. That is, and to the nondualist, God is not an external presence nor a personality; God is the Reality which permeates existence. Mankind, too, is God presently and temporarily occupying limited forms. In simple terms, God need not thank God for providing food to God. Further, to make the statement that "God is the food" is not meant to render God into an object — which is both an oversight and an impossibility — but rather to point to the fact that energy received from eating food in a conscious state of mind is divine and leads to the ability to recognize how energy is to be utilized for higher life and the realization of this divinity within.

So, this is the three-step process which will help reclaim a forgotten aspect of Kundalini Yoga, and of life in general. First, food is to be considered sacred, nothing less than God in the form of nature. Secondly, holy words are to be uttered over the food to both purify it of defects and render it into prasad, a sacred offering to the deities within. And third, the aspirant is to keep the mind still and focused while ingesting all meals, thinking within that the energy being produced by the partaking of food in a conscious manner is to be sublimated and brought "up the spine" to be utilized for spiritual purposes. The ancient Rishis of India knew these crucial elements, and followed them reverently. For instance, in the Taittiriya Upanisad it is stated: *"One should not disrespect food. It should be sanctified and observed as a pious rule. Life indeed is food. The body is the eater of food. The body is set in life; life is set in the body. Therefore, food is established in food. Those who contemplate food as being established in food, they themselves become firmly established. They become the enjoyer of food, producing an abundance of food for others, and command plenty of food."*

At this juncture, the practice of Kundalini Yoga enters a more esoteric phase, but only after the practical has been accounted for and one's daily thoughts and actions have been reclaimed from the realm of mundane habits and superficial preoccupations. The word used above, "sublimation," is one of the English language's most fitting words for our spiritual purposes here. The transformation of energy extracted from the intake of food into a more pure form, called *"mukhyaprana"* in Sanskrit, is a subtle one that cannot be described by ordinary modes of expression. It can only be felt upon the implementation of subtle techniques as are being described here. In brief, if one eats food while thinking mundane thoughts, or worse, talks about worldly subjects, or reads a murder mystery while partaking, the food and its energy get tainted. This is rather like preparing a sumptuous repast in the kitchen only to end up eating it in the bathroom. It is unthinkable; the two elements, act and location, are at odds. And such contradictions, especially when repeated over and over again, day after day, cannot help but to leave a perverse impression *(samskara)* on the mind, an unseen, unknown groove in the mind stuff *(chitta)* which carries over into the next incarnation.

But much different from this all-too-common scenario is the conscious elevation of the mind so that life-force, otherwise squandered or frittered away in ordinary or adverse ways, gets sublimated. This is not to say that using the energy one gets from food to engage in ordinary life is bad. It is rather to say that utilizing it for higher purposes is much more advantageous. In the case of food, it produces, among other things, a man's seed, which, when given to the future mother, helps produce the fetus. The point here is that if all the elements of this common process are done in higher awareness, a pure soul may choose to take birth. This is a great boon upon the parents, and a rare one in these times, especially in the West. But the energy which is stored up in a man or woman can also be utilized for higher learning, for artistic endeavors, and for raising a dharmic family. Kundalini Yoga's great gift, however, is in pointing out how to utilize the refined energy from food for evolving one's spiritual life. And this esoteric secret gets revealed in the succeeding stages of this practice.

As the chart on page four shows, the refined life-force called mukhyaprana is a perfect medium on which to mount the all-important element of spiritual practice *(sadhana)*. It is refined energy from food combined with spiritual disciplines like devotions, study of scriptures, selfless service, japa, and meditation, that cause the transformation of pranic energy into

Ojas, stored up spiritual power. The fortunate person who possesses mukhyaprana is ready to take such an inward trajectory. The unfortunate fact, however, is that of the many who reach this pinnacle of good health, most would rather, out of ignorance or willful intention, use this rarefied force only for outward activities that bring mere pleasure or an improved quality of physical life. And whereas this is certainly a "good" option considering the many negative alternatives possible, the downside of it is that what is "better" and "best" get overlooked. That is, "better" is performing spiritual disciplines (sadhana), and "best" is realizing the goal of human existence called *Samadhi*, or "Self-realization" in English.

To reclaim the unique Kundalini power that is always and originally one's own, the aspirant will have to work and operate a subtle inner alchemy which avows that energy from food, once it is purified and offered in sacrifice, can be stored up and sublimated. The result of this sublimation process, in and of itself, is a mystery — the only proof of it being the advent of inner experiences for which there are no logical explanations. When mukhyaprana and sadhana combine properly to equal ojas, the graduating aspirant begins to feel within the body/mind mechanism the presence of a singular and exceptional inner peace — *"The Peace that Passeth all understanding"* — that is tantamount to bliss.

The hurdle, here, is to forego fascination and obsession with such temporary and transitory states and conditions in lieu of arriving at the "Ocean of Bliss" — *Ananda Sagara* — which is the real object of one's search, and which is also one's own inner nature. The story given to warn and inform spiritual aspirants in this regard is of the man who, having just barely survived many days lost in the wilderness, suddenly breaks through the edge of the forest to stumble upon a sign with an arrow pointing towards civilization. He is so relieved and overjoyed at this that he wraps his arms around the sign and will not let go of it. Thus, he cheats himself of all the rich bounty that awaits him down the pathway a few miles. It is in this way that some beginning and intermediate seekers risk getting caught by a few experiences of conditioned joy and ephemeral elation that may well hamper progress along the spiritual path and arrival at its ultimate destination.

Ojas, rightly perceived and properly generated, is responsible, among other things, for awakening the aspirant to the presence of the *chakras*. These are spiritual centers held within the subtle and causal bodies, one of which courses beyond them and transcends them. These spiritual centers, or "lotuses" as they are sometimes called, are actually vortexes of spiritual energy which congeal and concentrate Kundalini force. Awareness of them by degrees, in sequence, means that the "straightening of one's coil" is actually taking place. This can be a complex process and holds room in it for both discovery and confusion. More on the chakras, including a few visuals, will be given in forthcoming pages. For now, suffice to say that the common explanation — that the chakras are somehow lodged in the human spine — is inadequate to the task of describing them and what they designate. In the *Srimad Devi Bhagavatam*, the Divine Mother's own scripture, the Devi states that these spiritual centers are interior realms with many levels and atmospheres, probably what Jesus was speaking of when He said *"The kingdom of Heaven lies within you,"* and *"My Father's Mansion has many chambers."* The esoteric descriptions of some of these realms will be excerpted from the scriptures and taken up and examined in other chapters. In the meantime, the human spine is to be utilized in meditation as a symbolic diagram, like a template, to help the mind envision what is entirely beyond the power of the body and senses to realize.

Returning to the phase of ojas and the storing up of spiritual power, it is after the onset of relative bliss is experienced and transcended that a certain preparedness visits the soul (psycho/physical being) and takes up residence there. The aspirant is now called an *Urdhvaretoyogi* — a newly arrived adept whose sublimated force is moving inwards (up the spinal column). We are to remember that this is all due to the principle of food and a fresh and welcome awareness of its true meaning, i.e., not for pleasure, or mere enjoyment of vital force, nor for survival. For again, *"Man does not live by bread alone"* or, as my Guru used to say, *"You must eat to live, not live to eat."* To put a finer point on this, there is conventional life, worldly life, sensual life, even demonic life; then there is dharmic life, divine life — even transcendence of life (*videhamukti*, or freedom from all bodies). Of all these choices the dedicated aspirant is courting the dharma first, which goes a step beyond morals and ethics. The meaning of food and what it signifies is going to be crucial in this endeavor, and important for comprehension of Kundalini Shakti, in the wise move towards mastering and utilizing it for the highest good of all.

It must be said that the term "food" has more to it than what has even been stated herein and thus far. Whereas beginning aspirants are very fond of stretching the body in physical yoga (*hatha*), it would be much better for them to mentally "stretch" the word "food" to glean its deeper significance. Everything that one takes into the body/mind mechanism is to be considered and included. In other words, there are different levels of food to work with: fruits, vegetables, and grains taken by the body; deep and prolonged amounts of oxygen taken consciously into the lungs; peaceful and inspiring scenes and sounds of nature taken in by the eyes, ears, and other senses; and especially, knowledge taken in by the mind. All of these are to be considered as different types of food, and all of them rendered pure by one's awakened and sharpened facility of intelligence. These kinds of sustenance are to be garnered by the novitiate within the scope of the subject of spiritualized food, and thereby all of these will be transmuted in the sublimation process by the Kundalini Yoga method (please refer to the appendix on food on page 85).

To complete the right hand column of the chart under

study on page four, the topic of *Tejas* next comes to the fore. Storing up power via the subtle process thus far described is not enough for the aspiring adept, or for the blossoming yogi or yogini. This concentrated power is certainly used to help them course further and deeper inwards in their ecstatic exploration of the many *lokas* within, but it also finds an outlet externally. This occurs when the illumined soul turns to help others along the path, from struggling aspirants to the suffering masses. Anywhere that the darkness of ignorance is still prevailing, there the luminary can shed a light — the light of refined Tejas — on person, place, or situation.

In this context, and as Swami Vivekananda has stated, principles are more important than people, so the luminary will adhere to and teach ignorance-destroying philosophical principles in all ways, at all times. But people as souls are more important than people as personalities (egos), and so the yogi and yogini adhering to the principles of Kundalini practice will turn the light of tejas upon students, family, children, and humanity in general to effect an overall positive result. The light of tejas, often literally shining from the very pores of the skin of the luminary, reduces suffering, lifts the spirit, transmits subtle wisdom, and destroys doubt and confusion in the minds of receptive people. It is this light — the living Kundalini Shakti — which all admire and adore, whether they know it or not, and not just the personality or personage of the luminary.

And here, at this refined level, is where the inner alchemy of Kundalini Yoga becomes less of a combination of distilled spiritualized ingredients and time-sensitive chemistry, and more of a living, breathing artform. The very principle of prana, life-force, including the physical food that contains it, can now be seen as nothing other than the Kundalini Shakti Herself. It is She, the Divine Mother of the Universe in the form of food, prana, mukhyaprana, ojas, and tejas, that subtly transforms into Kundalini Shakti right before the very "inner eye" (*Ajna chakra*) of the advanced devotee.

Here is the proper moment to bring in the advaitic axiom of *Sarvam Khalvidam Brahma*, "All is Brahman," as an apt correlation to this fundamentally Tantric medium. And, in fact, it might be fitting to say that Kundalini Shakti is the perfect blend (and the excellent marriage or reconciliation, if any be needed), of Tantra and Vedanta. And one might as well mix generous amounts of Yoga into the recipe as well. As Swami Vivekananda once intimated about Indian thought and philosophy, *Sankhya* is the body, *Tantra* is the heart, *Vedanta* is the brain, and *Yoga* is the practice and the proper course of action. Commingling these four in the kitchen of the aspiring soul is tantamount to full realization of the Truth. Quoting from the great Swami's letters in this regard, he stated wonderfully: "*I have clear light now, free of all hocus-pocus. I want to give Truth dry hard reason, softened in the sweetest syrup of love, and made spicy with intense work, and cooked in the kitchen of Yoga so that even a baby can easily digest it. I will compare Truth to a corrosive substance of infinite power. It burns its way in wherever it falls — in soft substance at once, hard granite slowly, but it must.*"

Switching our gaze to the left hand side of the chart under study on page four, we can take a practical look at the singular evolution that the practice of Kundalini Yoga provides for the sincere spiritual aspirant. Up the middle of the chart is a diagram showing the six chakras (the seventh, the *Sahasrara chakra*, is not really considered a "center") coinciding with the list in that column.

Of immediate note is the line of demarcation indicating a return to transmigratory existence in cycles. It corresponds with souls abiding ignorantly at the three lower chakras only — called *Muladhara*, *Svadhisthana*, and *Manipura*. Using the spine and body as a metaphoric template, we can correlate the lower three centers to eating, drinking, and sex life. Beings involved in mundane life gravitate here and rise no higher (deeper). The Kundalini force within them, then, is compacted drastically, and signs or leanings towards higher awareness are, unfortunately, seldom noticed. Christ's saying that one should not *"strew pearls before swine,"* slap in the face that it is, pertains here. As Sri Ramakrishna has stated, *"Even God is powerless to awaken them,"* speaking of those who are stuck deep in the mire of worldliness and its concomitants of lust, anger, greed, envy, pride, and delusion. Searching for an equivalent saying in English: *"Fools rush in where wise men fear to tread."* Statements such as these only serve to emphasize how dense the *maya* of delusion is amidst the denizens of these base realms.

As an important aside here it must be said that if we assume that systems like Kundalini Yoga and other salient Indian philosophies are pessimistic, or that they are not life-affirming, we will prematurely do them a grave injustice. Though they may not be "life-affirming," they are most definitely divine-life affirming and will afford those who are ready and willing to grow inwardly an avenue, or avenues, up and out of ignorance. For, to live totally unawares of the potential spiritual power lying dormant within is to live in outright ignorance. Religions from India, like Buddhism and others, have indicated such nescience by pointing to the cosmic phenomena of *Samsara* — rounds of birth and death in ignorance — engaged in by the masses. An escape from such a stunted lifestyle is both redeeming and freeing. No sensible person, once experiencing it, would deny divine life and trade it in for worldly existence. In constant touch with Mother Reality as Kundalini Shakti, and possessing an endless stream of convincing wisdom songs, the Bengali poet-saint, Ramprasad, cries out melodically, *"O idiotic mind, what misfortune you have brought upon yourself! You barter Her Golden Radiance at the center of your being for a fragmentary world of mere colored glass."*

The three lower chakras, interestingly enough, are the busy and bustling vortexes of transmigratory existence. All travel taking place as conjured-up projection in the mind-chariot, with the intellect as the guide and the ego along for the ride, happens predominantly among these three centers. And in fact, Sri Ramakrishna Paramahamsa has correlated the Seven Chakras of Kundalini Yoga with the Seven Lokas of Vedic cosmology (see chart on page 41). This would mean that the Muladhara, Svadhisthana, and Manipura chakras pertain to *Bhur, Bhuvar,* and *Svar lokas,* also corresponding roughly with earth, intermediary/ancestors, and heaven realms. This makes sense even in the context of the heaven of the Christians, wherein the soul transmigrates from heaven to earth, and even to hell, evidently. Whatever the case may be, in the Kundalini system it is via the three lower chakras that the soul (the subtle body consisting of unresolved thoughts and desires) enters and exits life in the embodied state.

But illumined souls pass in and out of the four higher chakras — *Anahata, Vishuddha, Ajna,* and *Sahasrara* — the four subtler centers shown in the diagram on the chart presently under study (page 4). It can be seen that when the soul strives to transcend mundane life at the Manipura chakra, all wrapped up and concerned with fear of loss, anxiety at getting and keeping (not losing), and emotionalism around matters of survival and relationships (see chart on page 31), it begins to perceive the light of wisdom and the sound of truth (*Jyoti* and *Omkara*). The Sanskrit term, *Anahata,* the name for the fourth chakra, is another word for *Om* (AUM), the "Unstruck Sound" of creation. It is when consciousness arrives here, as the left hand column on the chart reveals, that spiritual life really proceeds.

But prior to this we see that some spiritual awakening must take place, even if only to test the soul for readiness for higher life. Therefore, life at the Manipura chakra level is replete with early moral exercises, the type of which ethical people have been observing for lifetimes. The problem here is that many souls do not transcend this level, i.e., they remain good moral people but never gain liberation, only salvation. And that salvation itself, based on a presumed post mortem emancipation, is attended by mental travel between earth and heaven inexorably. In plain speech, this scenario corresponds to visiting the ancestor realm again and again, thus becoming an ancestor again and again. Thousands of souls, even whole countries, attend to this cycle based upon dualistic worship.

Interestingly enough, and as the *Yoga Kundalini Upanisad* points out, the Kundalini force of many aspiring souls is not residing predominantly in the Muladhara (base of the spine) anymore. It has uncoiled itself inwards into the Manipura chakra (solar plexus) and therein resides, looking to gain entrance into the Anahata (heart) regions. Some yogis have opined that the Unstruck Sound, Om, actually emanates from the Manipura, i.e., the navel. It seems to, but in actuality its residence is in the Anahata chakra, its namesake. It is in the Manipura that beings are getting an intimation of the presence of Om. And that is why, as the chart demonstrates, that early sadhana, refined prana, psychic prana, and the experience of *udghata* make themselves known there.

Udghata is a precursor to the rising of Kundalini force to the heart chakra. Just as a sound technician tests a microphone to see if the speakers are working, in similar fashion the Divine Mother Shakti tests the readiness of the soul at the level of the heart to see if it is ready to live at a more rarefied atmosphere. Experiences of subtle bliss, or cosmic revelation, and of increasing devotion, transpire here, all to test the preparedness of the soul for inner life. There are souls, after all, who, once experiencing udghata, imagine that they have reached the goal of realization. That remains to be seen. The question is, can they hold such heights when the gunas run their cycles in the mind? Usually not. Sri Ramakrishna's story in this regard is about the rare blue lotus which opens its petals to the sun, but when a cloud covers it the lotus cannot bear it and folds up again. Thus He once said, *"Even ordinary people can experience samadhi at times. But they cannot hold it for long."*

Real spiritual growth happens when the *Brahmanadi,* the mouth to the *Sushumna,* is opened. Sushumna is the central channel; *Ida* is the left side nadi, and *Pingala* is the right side nadi, designated on the image on the chart on page four. Real spiritual growth matures, however, when the *Vishnugranthi* is pierced, allowing Kundalini force into the heart, or Anahata chakra. Then, as the chart suggests, cycles of transmigration end and spiritual life proceeds, culminating in the piercing of the *Rudragranthi* just prior to the "third eye" chakra (Ajna). "*Granthi*" means "knot" in Sanskrit, so these three knots are closures in the Sushumna canal which must be thrown wide in order for Kundalini Shakti to course upwards (inwards) and unite with *Paramasiva* (Supreme Reality) at the crown of the head (Sahasrara). All of this esoteric description and knowledge is a part of the Kundalini Yoga way of expression, and should be well noted by the serious and sincere aspirant. Corroboration, of course, will take place by way of inner experience — the acid test in all of this. In the case of the practiced yogi, then, both death and rebirth are "turned on their ear." As the *Katha Upanisad* tells it, "*Hundred and one are the nerves of the inmost heart; of them, one has extended itself towards the crown of the head. Going upwards by it man attains immortality; but others depart differently.*"

Some of spiritual life's most beneficial attributes begin to show themselves at this juncture of inner practice. As the list on the chart reveals, maturing devotion, the cessation of fresh karmas, the ability to concentrate and meditate — such abilities as these are most welcome of attainment and are worlds of realization and experience in their own right. But Kundalini Shakti will not feel fulfilled in Her singular purpose if She does not penetrate beyond the Ajna chakra (third eye) and empty Her powerful river of pure, sentient Force into the boundless ocean of Paramasiva. Only He can contain Her, fulfill Her, delight Her. And only She can galvanize Him, otherwise static only, and convince Him to gravitate back down (through) the spiritual centers to bring and distribute the Light of pure, conscious Awareness there. Thus the Yantra of two diametrically opposing triangles which form a star, signifying the Shakti Force rising and the Siva Light falling.

In the meantime, though, and until that blissful union, further intensification is taking place. The fires of Yoga must become kindled to a white hot condition in order that *Sanchita karma*, unwanted subtle residue from previous actions in past lifetimes, gets annulled. These are hidden karmas, devastating where the attainment of Samadhi is concerned, and it takes some deep penetration to locate their hiding places in the sub-conscious mind, what to speak of even coming to know of their very existence. But their destruction allows for a ready and complete transmission of knowledge based in tejas, and entrance into an entirely unique realm of transcendental experiences, or seedless samadhis. This is designated on the chart on page 4 at the top by the term, *Ananda Ghana*, a mass of indeterminable Bliss. The aspirant, once a novice, then an adept, now a master, "rests" here, meaning that full immersion into the Ocean of Brahman is at hand. As Shankaracharya has written in his great scripture, *Vivekachudamani: "There within is the illimitable and ever-blissful ocean of Brahman, replete with the nectar-like swell of the Atman, into which my mind merged, like a hailstone falling into the sea...."*

The apt conclusion of this chart, and this chapter, is accented by the quote at the top of the chart by Sri Sarada Devi, the Holy Mother. Known, among other things, for Her pure and knowledgeable awareness around food and its ingestion, She tells us that pure food produces pure blood, and that pure blood results in pure thoughts. From here the way is open to Original Mind, sometimes called Buddha Mind or Pure Mind. Unmodified Intelligence may be another way of saying this, which smacks of Kundalini Shakti's way of proceeding. May this wholly unique procedure, the straightening of the coil of utmost human potential, initiate itself in this lifetime and lend divine expression to all of existence, in all realms, and at all levels of Awareness.

≈ 2 ≈

Mental Posture and Informed Breathing

Asana and Pranayam in Tantric Yoga

Once the sincere spiritual aspirant has been prepared for entrance into spiritual life by such indispensible preliminaries as the yamas and niyamas (truthfulness; nonviolence in thought, word and deed; purification; chastity, austerity, study, devotions, etc.), then only is he fit to assume yogic posture. With grounding of this nature no wayward or misleading thoughts or intentions will disturb his precious but sensitive mental equilibrium. For, it takes resolve of the highest order to both withstand and transcend all that will come up and to the fore in phases that are to follow — phases which will find the seeker dealing with everything from the six passions and the eight fetters, right on in to the hidden samskaras and karmas from past lives that cause dalliance with these unwanted despoilers. And it is the unfortunate case, especially in modern western countries among novitiates and beginners who are encountering all forms of eastern thought, that qualification is not sought and attained prior to the conscious acts of sitting, breathing, and meditating. That is why the rate of failure is so high, and success (enlightenment) almost nonexistent.

The Twenty Yamas and Niyamas of Tantra

"I am the World Mother. Fix heart and mind upon this lustrous Form of Mine and soon you will realize the union of Jiva and Brahman." **Sri Devi**

AHIMSA
Nonviolence

SATYAM
Truthfulness

ASTEYAM
Non-stealing

BRAHMACHARYA
Sense-Control

Ten Yamas

DAYA
Compassion

SAMATVA
Steadiness

DRITI
Firmness

AKARTRTVAMA
Moderation

KSHAMA
Forgiveness

SAUCHA
Purity

TAPASYA
Austerity

DANAM
Charity

TUSHTI
Contentment

SHRADDHA
Faith in Dharma

ASTIKYA
Faith in Scripture

HOMA
Sacrificial Oblations

Ten Niyamas

HRI
Modesty

ISHVARA-PUJANAM
Worship of God

SIDDHANTAVAKYA-SHRAVANA
Study & Confirmation of Scriptures

JAPA
Mantra

"The enemies to Yoga, union with the Self, are the six passions — lust, anger, greed, ignorance, vanity, and jealousy. The practitioner overcomes them by the attainment of the Eight Limbs of Yoga, and does so by first practicing and accomplishing limbs one and two — the Ten Yamas and the Ten Niyamas." **Sri Devi**

The facing page shows a chart created from the words of the Divine Mother of the Universe spoken in Her scripture, the *Srimad Devi Bhagavatam*, illustrating Her cogent advice in the form of no less than twenty prerequisites which are to be sought after early in one's spiritual practice.

If we inspect these twenty practices we can see the import that the Goddess places upon setting the ground for spiritual life. This chart also mentions the passions that occupy the minds of embodied beings in much the same way that wasps nest in an old tree truck. Yet, these pose little problem to those who observe the initial practice of yamas and niyamas given by the preceptors and the scriptures. The oft seen problem in the West among its yogic practitioners of simply giving up one's practice is due to the student being unable to master the requisites listed here. Mistakes such as the arrogance of thinking that one knows better than one's guru, and the tendency and temptation to jump steps based upon a premature and exaggerated sense of one's own status and abilities, are common signs of spiritual immaturity. With the Divine Mother Herself listing out the best regimen for Her acolytes, these sincere and persevering devotees go forward along the path and do not betray the faith of the wise teachers. Nor do they ever and thereby detract from the dharma and its ironclad principles. This is a word to the wise from the spiritual preceptor, received directly via the words of the Wisdom Goddess in the Mother scriptures.

With this important bit of information transmitted, the topics of *asana* and *pranayam* can be taken up. True Kundalini Yoga adherents do not fixate on these two elements, but simply use them to pave the way towards higher and deeper levels of consciousness. Others, who wish for health of the body, pleasures of the flesh, life of the senses, longevity, occult powers, and the like, are seen to gravitate to these two aspects with a penchant bordering on obsession. Taking this improvident route, very soon the honorable institution of Yoga will be torn from its lofty perch as the definitive spiritual discipline in action, and rendered a caricature of itself in the eyes of whole nations and masses of onlookers. Of all the many calamities of this day and time this is certainly one of the most lamentable, for maintaining the institution of Yoga at the high level that it is meant to exist will help school the future luminaries of this world and provide protection and sustenance for spiritual life. Otherwise, the subtle wonders of the mind and spirit will be lost again, to whole cultures — *"over the long efflux of time"* as Sri Krishna states — and the darkness of ignorance of the true Self of mankind will win the day once again. This darkness, in this day and age, is cited by such words as worldliness, delusion, and materialism. It is a more devious opponent than evil, for evil is easy of detection compared to the ingredients of ignorance: weakness, pretense, forgetfulness, and apathy.

The secret of success as far as true yogic adepts are concerned, and the reason that they are able to sit easily and comfortably without undue strain and effort, is the assumption of an informed *mental* posture before sitting. Just as a psychological edge is present and utilized in so many earthly endeavors, the same is true in the practice of Yoga. As an artist would envision a painting on a blank canvas before setting his brush to it, or a pujari would mentally assess and gather all elements for a ritualistic ceremony before actually undertaking it, just so will the informed yoga practitioner set his asana in the mind before settling in to meditate. Unlike the hatha yogi, this is not an envisioning of what position he is going to assume next; that is already accomplished — ekasana, the one posture that is best for meditation. Rather, the mental attitude is what is being established, and well in advance of the forthcoming act.

This is why advanced meditators eventually never leave meditation, even when moving about. As Holy Mother has said, *"Does God exist only when the eyes are closed, but cease to exist when eyes are open?"* Prior to the ability to meditate throughout life in all its phases, the consummate practitioner maintains the "asana of meditation" in his mind as he leaves his seat at night, and holds and projects it in advance of his meditation the next morning. The whole affair is seamless, wherein one continuous flow of focused awareness runs uniformly and free of interruption between the mover and the Immovable, the lover and the Beloved, the meditator and the Meditated. This is real asana. All else, as Shankara has said, is merely *"the twisting and torturing of the limbs."*

This holds true of breathing exercises as well. They can be a mere bellows-like inflation and deflation of the lungs in order to effect a little pleasant dizziness in the head; or they can be a way to slow the heart rate; or they can usher in the silent observance of rhythmic in-breath and out-breath in controlled cycles; or they can be a way of settling the mind and besting restlessness. But the wisest among us have indicated a secret to the breathing process, much like to food and its conscious consumption as explained in the first chapter of this book.

Informed pranayama, like asana, is born of initial practices such as the yamas and niyamas. Studying the scriptures (svadhyaya), for instance, places one in knowledge of what the three phases of the breathing process signify philosophically. Mating the in-breath, *puraka*, with the first matra of AUM, "A," duly connects manas (mind), chitta (thoughts), ahamkara (ego), and buddhi (intellect), to awareness of the world as being a product of one's own thinking process, and gives the practitioner license to explore and conquer that world — to reclaim it as an extension of the Self, Atman.

In this regard, the predicament of modern man, even for millennia, has been that he has not known that the mind creates the world; he attributes it to some imagined creator. In this case, he projects the world out of his mind, with all its forms and objects, then forgets his part in this dream-like act and ends up a slave to the very objects he projected, falling further into suffering when he cannot grasp and hold onto these solid figments of his own mental process. Grasping objects made of minute particles, all changing at a rate of a billionth of a second, is rather like trying to hold water or air in one's hands. Objects are mental fabrications made of dream stuff, projected vibration congealed, soon to break apart again. No wise person would attempt to own them indefinitely.

In the same way that integrating the in-breath with the A of AUM connects one to realization of the true relationship of the soul with the outer world, similarly does marrying the suspended breath (kumbhaka) with the "U" of AUM open and reveal the inner world, or subtle world, to the meditator. What was previously considered a mere field of dreams without any basis suddenly becomes an interior realm that is more real, i.e., closer to the Infinite Being, than the waking state. The meditator, watching his breath in this informed mode, brooks the experience of perceiving the source of all projected phenomena lying within the mind-scape, like so many precious jewels strewn across an ocean floor. The internal worlds get lit up, and breathing, what to speak of meditation, is no longer an exercise in calming the mind; it is more a matter of revelation.

The final willful act of the involved meditator in this triune process is the commingling of the out-breath (rechaka) with the matra "M" of AUM. The consonant, "M," brings an end to words, just as the out-breath signals an end to the cycle of one complete pranayam. The word, "end," here is used in regards to an end to form and movement, a merging into what is formless and eternal. This matra has been aligned philosophically with the deep sleep state of the human being, where waking and dreaming both dissolve. This state is formless, yet begs exploration with the newly opened inner eye of Awareness — the *Jnana Chakshu.* Seers know this state as the doorway to divinity, which remains closed to all those who remain uninformed of the interior connections taught here. There will be more information on the Jnana chakshu in forthcoming chapters. For now, the reader is invited to view the many meanings of AUM on the chart on the facing page.

Om & Hrim — The Two Great Bijas

"One should go into the region where there is no speech or thing spoken, absolutely free from dualities — Akhanda Satchitananda. There, with Aum, meditate on that Highest Flame of Consciousness. In this rare meditation great beings have destroyed ignorance, realized their perfect Nature, and established identity of the Jiva with Brahman. This is My Highest Self!" — Srimad Devi Bhagavatam

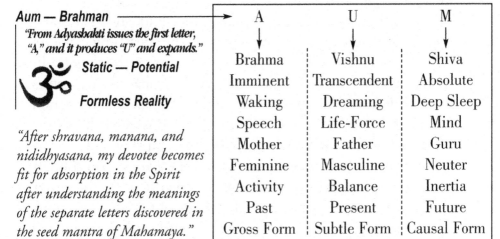

Aum — Brahman

"From Adyashakti issues the first letter, "A," and it produces "U" and expands."

Static — Potential

Formless Reality

"After shravana, manana, and nididhyasana, my devotee becomes fit for absorption in the Spirit after understanding the meanings of the separate letters discovered in the seed mantra of Mahamaya."

A	U	M
Brahma	Vishnu	Shiva
Imminent	Transcendent	Absolute
Waking	Dreaming	Deep Sleep
Speech	Life-Force	Mind
Mother	Father	Guru
Feminine	Masculine	Neuter
Activity	Balance	Inertia
Past	Present	Future
Gross Form	Subtle Form	Causal Form

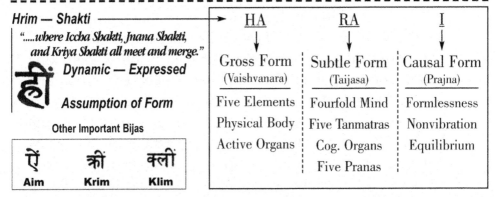

Hrim — Shakti

".....where Iccha Shakti, Jnana Shakti, and Kriya Shakti all meet and merge."

Dynamic — Expressed

Assumption of Form

Other Important Bijas

ऐं — Aim   श्रीं — Krim   क्लीं — Klim

HA	RA	I
Gross Form (Vaishvanara)	Subtle Form (Taijasa)	Causal Form (Prajna)
Five Elements	Fourfold Mind	Formlessness
Physical Body	Five Tanmatras	Nonvibration
Active Organs	Cog. Organs	Equilibrium
	Five Pranas	

*"After balancing the breath via pranayama, and cognizing the differentiated states of the bija-mantra and what they signify, meditate on that bija and mentally dissolve the gross body into the subtle body, the subtle body into the causal body, and then the causal body into the Turiya state of Hrim symbolized by the matra **M**. And before entering Samadhi, focus upon Me, the Supreme Deity, the luminous, Self-effulgent Goddess who is one with Brahman."* — Srimad Devi Bhagavatam

The chart on the next facing page, page 27, schools us in the basics of asana and pranayama once we have been informed by the teachings just given. In the area of sitting positions per se, the yogis tend to focus on five basic postures as given in the scriptures. Briefly, the lotus and half lotus, the heroic, the auspicious, and the diamond seat are well liked by all traditional meditators.

With regards to pranayama, the chart shows a small graph that teaches the art of increasing the breathing capacity by "four digits," meaning, in part, four counts on the fingers. If, upon experimenting (under the guru's supervision), one's breath is found to be shallow, the lungs of small capacity, then a regimen of practice focusing on expansion is needed. As per the chart's instructions, the practitioner begins by concentrating on the left nostril and envisioning the *Ida nadi* on the left side of the spine. If one is only able to breathe in for the count of eight, then an expansion to the count of twelve is attempted. The same is true of the held breath and the expelled breath. With practice, the student can work up to a 16 count cycle on each phase of the breath, maybe more, always being careful not to overheat and thus imbalanced the brain.

Speaking again of being informed before undertaking practices of this nature, the scriptures explain that when one increases the breathing count by four digits, one is to envision that these digits are expanding back into inner space, the akasha. This is an esoteric secret almost totally overlooked by contemporary hatha yoga practitioners. As taught previously, it is not only the waking state, but also the dreaming and deep sleep states that are a part of our soul's infinite territories — A, U, and M. They are to be reclaimed.

One thus becomes more aware of the subtle and causal worlds within when one extends the life breath, thus awareness of the life force (prana), back into them. Therefore, it is not for the student to merely sit and breathe, or even just watch the breath; this is elementary practice. Increasing the mind's

Asana & Pranayam in Tantric Yoga

"Hold the prana on the various parts of the body in turn — toes, heels, knees, thighs, chest, head, etc., — and practice pratyahara. Concentrating the mind on the Consciousness within is then made easier, and formal dharana will mature when the jivatma places the Istam inside."   King Himalaya

Phase	Locale	Channel	Beginner	Advanced
Inbreath ⟶	Left Nostril ⟶	Ida ⟶	12 Count ⟶	16 Count
Retained ⟶	Central ⟶	Sushumna ⟶	12 Count ⟶	64 Count
Outbreath ⟶	Right Nostril ⟶	Pingala ⟶	12 Count ⟶	32 Count

Three Stages of Pranayam
3) Highest Order: Mental Aspiration
2) Middling Order: Trembling
1) Lowest Order: Perspiration

Sagarbha Pranayam
Pranayama performed
with japa and meditation
on the Ishtam

Vigarbha Pranayam
Pranayama performed
while repeating the bijam
Om

Padmasana
(Lotus pose)

Svastikasana
(Auspicious pose)

Bhadrasana
(Beneficial pose)

Vajrasana
(Diamond pose)

Virasana
(Heroic pose)

The Five
Essential Asanas

*"These five body positions
are very much liked by the
adept yogis, who advise
their practice in everyday
sadhana."* King Himalaya

awareness of what lies within is the "thread that connects to the string that ties to the rope." In this informed practice, both the inner realms (lokas) and all that impedes the meditator from coursing through those lands, will open up for scrutiny, the end result being what is called "enlightenment." The advaitic axiom, *"Thou art That"* means to convey that every strata of consciousness and every shred of awareness within them, right on up to the Ultimate Reality, is within the Soul. Ignorance, many lifetimes long, consists of not knowing this fact, and this ignorance has its seat in the mind of mankind. Devils and demons lie there — not as independently existing incarnate evils, but as projections of the human mind in ignorance, inclusive of all of its many deceptions and delusions.

Here, the real focus of Yogic practice comes to the fore; it is the mind. Remove its foibles and dharmic life will ensue. Remove it entirely and realization of the formless is at hand, is unavoidable. The *Yoga Kundalini Upanisad* begins on this powerful note, incorporating what is needful of hearing in order to place the aspirant on sure footing from the outset:

"The ordinary mind's thoughts have two causes: desires and the prana. If one of them is controlled, both are controlled. To master the prana one requires pure and nutritious food taken in a conscious and moderate manner, and the mastering of the padma and vajra asanas. When ready, the aspirant is then to recognize the shakti force within and take it up from its place at the manipura to the middle of the eyebrows. By the practice of pranayama under the guidance of a guru, and the worship of the Goddess who is none other than Kundalini, one's coil, which is spiral, becomes straightened. This is a great mystery...."

A further "informing" of the pranayam is received when the student takes up discipleship with a spiritual preceptor in a particular lineage of a religious tradition. The newborn acolyte receives what is called *mantra-diksha,* or the transmission of the mantra from *guru* to *shishya.* As the chart on the preceding page (27) illustrates, the breathing exercises become increasingly powerful when either the mantra is added to it, or the word of Brahman, AUM, is included. The first is called *Sagarbha Pranayam*, wherein repetition of the mantra is performed with every count of the in-breath, suspended breath, and expelled breath. The *Ishtam*, the "Chosen Ideal" selected for meditation on God with form, is also envisioned in this form of pranayam. When well performed, the effects are earth shattering, literally, as the world of name and form will dissolve into the Ishtam, or Cosmic Mind. As Swami Vivekananda has written in one of his poems honoring his own Guru, *"We shall crush the stars to atoms, we shall unhinge the universe. Don't you know who we are? We are the children of Sri Ramakrishna."*

The other form of pranayama is called *Vigarbha*. It is best for approaching formless meditation, or meditation on God without form. The bijam, AUM, is utilized with every count of the cycle of breathing. When pranayam of the lower order is accomplished it is said to bring heat and perspiration. When it is accomplished at the middling level a certain trembling, both of the body and the nerves, occurs. When the level of the highest order is reached, pure aspiration attends the mind. This is tantamount to getting ahold of the upward moving prana which, when unleashed, carries the mind into pellucid flights of intellectual, philosophical, and spiritual comprehension. Mother Kundalini as the Goddess Sarasvati loves that atmosphere, and there is no end to revelation there.

When all the elements which have been discussed in the first two chapters of this book have become foundational, and a sadhaka's practice is set up around them on a firm basis, experiences at the various levels of consciousness begin to transpire. As has been mentioned, these levels are called chakras in the Kundalini Yoga system, also "centers" and "lotuses." They are really spiritual vortexes within the marvelous human form, operating at subtle and causal levels of Awareness. A study of these will be undertaken next.

≈ 3 ≈

Nectars and Poisons

Aids and Impediments in the Kundalini Yoga System

As an introduction to the chakras, the six (or seven, if one counts the Sahasrara) spiritual vortexes which congeal and conduct Kundalini Shakti, this chapter will be given to examining the positive and negative attributes associated with each of these centers. The chart on the facing page will give us a first look at a diagram that illustrates them. And as the quote and teachings at the top of the chart reveal, all the rules of classic Yoga are in operation in the Kundalini Yoga system as well. Like Patanjali's Eight-limbed Yoga, there are a host of impediments which the aspirant has to watch out for.

The mind-set of a raja yogi is also similar, for any challenge, impediment, disease, obstacle, etc., is to be seen as a test rather than a calamity; or, as the Vedanta would explain it, as ultimately unreal. Therefore, the yogi relegates all changes, whatever may be their character, to nature and to the body, not to the Self or Soul. Nonreaction is thus the key word and the fundamental practice all in one. To react under undue circumstances, to any adverse occurrence in body, nature, life, or mind, is to risk the foundations of a yogi's practice tumbling down in chaos around his ears. As Sri Krishna teaches in the Bhagavad Gita, "*All changes in nature abide with the gunas of*

The Seven Causes & Ten Impediments in Kundalini Yoga

"Imbalances appear in the body due to several causes. If the yogic aspirant reacts to these then fears arise, and he falsely believes that his yogic practice has instigated these diseases. This is the first obstacle to the practice of Kundalini Yoga, so the yogi should abandon this and all other obstacles."   Yoga Kundalini Upanisad

Seven Causes		Ten Impediments	
Daytime Lassitude	Untimely Elimination of Waste	Reaction to Disease	Attachment to Objects
Nighttime Excesses		Doubt	Erroneous Perception
	Unwholesome Food	Carelessness	Oversensuality
Unchecked Sexuality		Laziness	Faithlessness
Frequenting Crowds	Erratic Condition of Prana and Mind	Sleep	Failure to Attain Truth

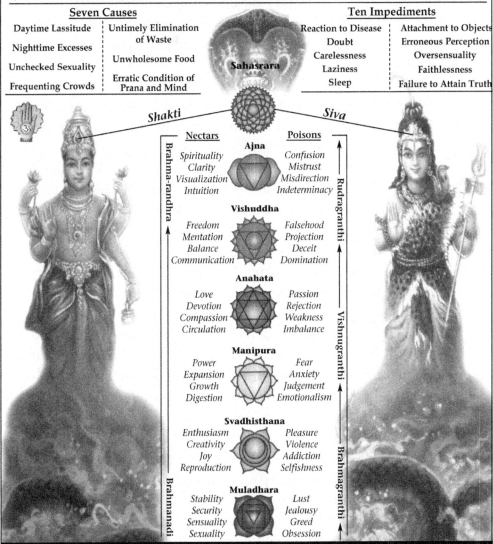

Sahasrara

Shakti   *Siva*

Brahma-randhra

— Nectars —   — Poisons —

Ajna

Nectars	Poisons
Spirituality	Confusion
Clarity	Mistrust
Visualization	Misdirection
Intuition	Indeterminacy

Rudragranthi

Vishuddha

Freedom	Falsehood
Mentation	Projection
Balance	Deceit
Communication	Domination

Anahata

Love	Passion
Devotion	Rejection
Compassion	Weakness
Circulation	Imbalance

Vishnugranthi

Manipura

Power	Fear
Expansion	Anxiety
Growth	Judgement
Digestion	Emotionalism

Svadhisthana

Enthusiasm	Pleasure
Creativity	Violence
Joy	Addiction
Reproduction	Selfishness

Brahmagranthi

Muladhara

Stability	Lust
Security	Jealousy
Sensuality	Greed
Sexuality	Obsession

Brahmanadi

"The Kundalini dwells in the Muladhara chakra. When it is aroused it passes along the Sushumna nerve, pierces the six centers, and at last reaches the lotus at the head, the Sahasrara. This is called the movement of the Mahavayu, the Spiritual Current, and it culminates in Samadhi. All the lotuses then blissfully blossom forth. This is a very secret experience." Sri Ramakrishna Paramahamsa

nature, and take place in nature only. *They do not take place in the Soul, the Purusha.*" This nondual mindset strengthens the body/mind mechanism substantially, what to speak of the yogi's unmatched resolve around reaching enlightenment. Change is apparent only. Reality is changeless, transformationless. Set upon this sterling maxim of spiritual life, the practice of the consummate yogi moves forward inexorably towards the Goal Supreme.

An interesting fact about the chakras of the Kundalini Yoga system is that they have inherent characteristics within them, all balanced to one another. Taking, for instance, the *Muladhara chakra* at the root of the spine, the first and "lowest" chakra, a more contemporary look at it (page 31) reveals that it contains the basest of passions on one side, yet some foundational building blocks of existence on the other. Though there are other delineations of the human passions to consider in accord with the spiritual centers, like in the *Shinay* (*"Burning pillar"*) system of meditation in Tibetan Buddhism, in the Kundalini Yoga view any given chakra might contain several of the human passions, though predominance could rest with one in particular, shifting with regard to any given individual. Thus here, at the Muladhara, lust, greed and jealousy all collide and mix in an unsavory manner, demonstrated adequately by the gross behavior of living beings who gravitate to and operate on this base center of existence alone.

On the other hand, under the "nectars" column on the left hand side of the chart (page 31), such mainstays as human sexuality, sensuality, security, and stability are present in this *mula,* or "basement" level chakra. To render all of this information more comprehendable is to explain that if the human being is sleeping to his or her spiritual potential, the poisons are predominant in life and activities, often with disastrous results. But when the soul is awake to Kundalini force, not only are grounding benefits such as stability and security accessible, the poisons found in the Muladhara level get purified and their power for benefit utilized for spiritual ascent. According to Sri Ramakrishna, the superlative modern Kundalini master, this is rather like defanging and removing the poison ducts of a cobra so that it can be handled easily, and impressively. In short, descending to the Muladhara chakra is not a risky matter for one who has "straightened his coil" and perceived the internal realms of existence. Some masters can and will descend into this potentially darksome area of human consciousness just to awaken and save suffering souls.

The reader is invited to study the diagram of the seven chakras, both from the bottom up and the top down, thereby gathering information which may be helpful for spiritual practice and advancement. The studious soul will thereby notice that there is a representative of each area of human consciousness in each chakra, i.e., the physical, vital, psychological, and intellectual. All that is needed for advancement, spiritually speaking, is there, dualistically complemented by all that invites failure as well.

In the *Svadhisthana chakra*, generally associated with the sexual organs, a veritable riot act of information makes itself known. Poisons and nectars constrict and flow there, either impeding the aspirant's spiritual ascent or restricting it as the case may be — all in accord with the existing abilities, or lack thereof, of any given practitioner. But the practiced yogi is used to challenges and utilizes them to increase both strength and resolve for the mastery of his awareness. From the earliest phases of practice — from taking food and its energy, to sensing its pranic content, to refining that content into stored up power, and on towards sublimating that power into spiritual force — all has been a testing ground, even on the subtlest of levels. In short, the consummate practitioner becomes accustomed to seeing and encountering dualities, but is bound and determined to transcend them.

At the *Manipura chakra* level, generally and physically correlated with the navel area, potential waxes strong. The

Yoga Kundalini Upanisad makes interesting mentions of the difference between those who are dwelling at the lowest chakra only, and those whose Kundalini power has risen to the Manipura and is fixed there for a time. Many beings, those who are more experienced in life and are beginning to see beyond its limitations, are existing mainly in this third chakra, this "vital" center of consciousness. This means that not only are they rising above the baser passions and fetters associated with the lower chakras, they are also beginning to storm the portals of the fourth, the *Anahata chakra*, the heart center.

Whereas life lived at the level of the Manipura chakra suffers negativities such as fear and anxiety, it also sees growth and expansion of its own powers around early mastery of matters relating to health and relationships. It is fitting, then, that those who are feeling, bringing forth, and expanding their aspirations would desire passage into the realm of the heart, and begin developing qualities that are characteristic of that refined inner arena.

But there is a solid reason why spiritual evolution gets stymied at this juncture. Immaturities concerning emotionalism, insincerity, aversion, and the like, hold the soul back and retard its inner progress; for none will enter the kingdom of the heart without abandoning the likes of these. Another way of saying this surfaces in teachings involving the Kundalini philosophy itself. The *Yoga Kundalini Upanisad* makes mention of a complex *"granthi"* at this juncture, a veil, knot, or subtle barrier between the Manipura and the Anahata chakras, mentioned earlier. It is called *Vishnugranthi*. Gaining hold of the spiritual wind, called (maha) vayu, or prana, and subjecting it to and commingling it with *agni*, the fire of intensification (sadhana), the aspirant breaks through this cosmic impediment and rises in spiritual stature and realization.

The first of these great knots, called *Brahmagranthi*, was already pierced earlier when the aspirant penetrated the opening at the base of the Sushumna nadi at the Muladhara chakra level. At a more refined level, then, this second great knot has to be pierced, opening human consciousness to wonders previously unseen. Soon, when the forehead chakra is broached, the *Rudragranthi*, a knot separating the throat chakra and the third eye chakra from the Sahasrara, will have to be dissolved. These three great knots, granthis, are also sometimes allocated to the three gunas of tamas, rajas, and sattva, respectively. They are to be transcended before full realization can be attained. To quote this Upanisad, *"Kundalini, heated up by Agni and stirred by Vayu, extends Her Force into the mouth of the Sushumna, pierces the Brahmagranthi formed of tamas and rajas, flashing like lightning in that aperture. Then it goes up through the Vishnugranthi at the heart and, not stopping there, penetrates the Rudragranthi above it, passing through the middle of the eyebrows."*

Like all things in relativity, the heart chakra is still subject to poisons. The chart on page 31 lists weakness, rejection, a general overall state of passion, and a tendency towards losing one's balance, as problems here. Thankfully, the aspirant can water the flowers instead of the weeds by relying upon the presence of sterling attributes like love and devotion. These are to be cultivated and expanded, the poisons transformed. The transmutation of poison into nectar is, in fact, one of Kundalini Yoga's most sublime of secrets and abilities.

The Wisdom center, called *Vishuddha chakra*, aligned physically with the throat, heralds one of burgeoning consciousness' most remote outposts. The Kundalini Shakti loves to sport here. As has already been explained, but worthy of reminder, the description of the chakras in accord with specific areas of the physical body and spine is only symbolic of what is really being indicated. As the chart on page 41 reveals, these spiritual centers lie within the inner reaches of Consciousness, not in matter. As the commentators of the Tantras state, *"The chakras are not perceptible to the gross senses. Even if they were present in the physical body, which they help to organize, they would only disappear with the disintegration of it upon its death."*

A study of the Three Worlds (material, subtle, and causal) and the Three Bodies (stula, sukshma, and karana), from the ancient Sankhya of Lord Kapila on to the more recent exposition in the Vedanta by Shankara is necessary for fuller comprehension of this fact. Classic Yoga, too, has these crucial subdivisions, from the linga (formed) to the alinga (formless) — the manifest to the unmanifest to the Supremely Unmanifest. Those who try to turn Kundalini Yoga into a system for physical health only leave out its most beneficial and enlightening levels. The chakras are inner realms, levels of seamless and homogenous Consciousness, and their discovery prove that beyond the world of atomic particles there are atmospheres which defy commonly held beliefs and concepts around the principles of time, spatiality, and dimension.

The chakra correlated with the throat, then, is where a taste of full freedom is gained. Communications here are of the loftiest nature — or can be if the poisons of deceit and domination do not gain the upper hand. Other negativities present here range from the insinuation of outright falsehood, to the appearance of confusion and the habit of projectionism (sankalpa/vikalpa). Thus, there is a fine line between an authentic wisdom seer and those who know much but use their knowledge for name, fame, and gain. The world always sees many fine orators, and a host of self-proclaimed teachers. But a complete mastery of the Vishuddha chakra demands several basic attributes, ones like humility, honesty, and the desire to serve selflessly. This chakra is also famous for being the hub for the neutralization of collective karmas, or what is often spoken of in Christianity as "vicarious atonement." It contains not just knowledge, but wisdom that destroys ignorance. Thus, it is a deep and refreshing well of mercy and forgiveness.

The chakra at the forehead, called the *Ajna chakra*, is perhaps the most famous of all. Termed the "Third Eye" in contemporary times, its presence has been so thoroughly intuited throughout time, despite the esoteric nature of its charac-

ter, that mentions of it appear in at least seven or eight different religious traditions of the world. More will be taught about
it later, with a chart provided (see page 47) to enhance the
telling. For now, suffice to say that its qualities on the positive
side include the valued attributes of clarity of vision and pure
spirituality. The power for deep and true visualization — a
type of pure omniscience — is also inherent in it.

On the other side, its light is so refined, so overwhelm-
ing when detected, that aspirants not yet ready for its singular
infusion can suffer confusion and misdirection amounting to a
fall from the spiritual path. For the uninitiated and unprepared, the light of the Ajna chakra light stuns, sending unqualified souls into a state of shock and indeterminacy. Many cases
of this deviation have come to the fore when instructions coming from the spiritual preceptor are ignored by over-enthusias-
tic students who, instead of meditating on the heart chakra
(Anahata) until consciousness is fully established there, focus
in the third eye region, losing proper direction and becoming
disoriented. This is also what transpires in those all too familiar cases of spiritual pretenders and charlatans, many of them
well-known and attended by many beguiled followers.
Premature occupation of the Ajna chakra by the as yet spiritually inept soul, or the one desirous of power and domination, is
cause for all manner of error and resultant suffering, both for
the perpetrators and their associates. Cases on contemporary
record include misuse of power, utilization of occult powers,
spurious acts ending in outrage and scandal, sexual miscon-
duct, the breaking of vows, and compromising the noble spiritual path via undue manipulation in the arenas of business,
politics, and other worldly matters, to name a few.

The remainder of the chart under study (page 31) has to
do with the problematic Seven Causes (for diseases) and the
Ten Impediments. As to both these sets, interconnected as
they are, it has long been known in India that all diseases are
of the mind. The thinking process has everything to do with

how the body lives. Even the breathing process is regulated by
the mind, though many do not know it. This is the reason why
the novitiate is asked to "become aware of the breath" in meditation. This is simply making the mind aware that the body
breathes, and by doing this, all else, i.e., burgeoning awareness
and its benefits, will follow naturally. Ultimately, the primordial disease which is the cause of all other illnesses, that of
rebirth in ignorance of one's true nature, is also of the mind.
As the wise saying goes, "*No mind, no matter. No matter?
Never mind.*"

The *Yoga Kundalini Upanisad* tells this story in no uncertain terms. Fear of disease in the mind transfers to the body in
the form of illness. Illness in the body transfers back to
thoughts of disease in the mind, leaving impressions there.
These and many other kinds of impressions, called *samskaras*,
persist in the mind even into succeeding lifetimes and are the
reason why people are born as they are and act as they do. But
living beings are not aware of these subtle causes of their
embodied existence. These impressions are hidden facets,
Vicchinavastha, and can only be uncovered by the combination
of a desire to awaken, the discovery of a spiritual guide, and
one's own persistent spiritual practice. Thereafter, some sense
is finally made out of this life lived in relativity. Everything —
habits, tendencies, instincts, genealogy, heredity — all that
modern medicine, science, and psychology are talking about
and experimenting with, positive, negative, and mixed —
spring from these samskaras formulated in past lives. Thus it is
written, inclusive of previous existences: "*Diseases are generated in the body through the following causes: sleeping in the daytime
(lethargy); late night vigils; excess of sexual intercourse; frequenting
crowds; undue checking of the discharge of urine and feces; the evil
of taking unwholesome food; and the imbalances of prana in the
mind. If the yogi fears and reacts to such diseases when attacked by
them, and thinks to himself falsely, 'These diseases have arisen from
my practice of Yoga,' then he will discontinue his practice.*"

This faulty conclusion is the first impediment, and thus is the connecting point between the causes and their effects. From there, as the scripture declares: *"The second obstacle is doubt; the third is carelessness; the fourth, laziness; the fifth, sleep; the sixth, failure to detach from the objects of the senses; the seventh, erroneous perception; the eighth, over indulgence in sense objects; the ninth, lack of faith; and the tenth, falling back and away from the attainment of Yoga's final end, samadhi. The wise seeker should abandon these ten after deep deliberation."*

As sterling and foundational as morals and ethics are, the wisdom precepts of the eternal dharma, put into action via spiritual practice, are far superior. Human nature as it is, riddled with errors and transgressions formulated around these seven causes listed above and further crystallized by these ten impediments, requires a far more concentrated purifying agent than a once a week attendance in church, a once a day vote of thanks at mealtime, and a once a night prayer before sleep. For seekers of truth in this darksome age, then, the powerful word, "*sadhana*," is of utmost import. The four classic Yogas of wisdom (jnana), devotion (bhakti), meditation (dhyana/raja), and selfless action (karma) define the word well. The traditional sadhaka chants the names of the Lord and Mother and repeats the mantra, studies and reflects upon the revealed scriptures and commits them to memory, meditates on God with form and beyond form, and performs all work as worship in service of God in mankind. The Seven Causes and Ten Impediments find no foothold in the sincere and sedulous seeker who maintains such an ongoing practice.

At the bottom of the chart on page 31 is a quote by Sri Ramakrishna. His personal spiritual experiences, as related in the unique book, *The Gospel of Sri Ramakrishna*, mention the chakras. With what has been declared thus far, enough of a foundation has been laid to enable a further presentation of the chakras in a more detailed and meditative manner — all leading to deep communion with the Kundalini Shakti Herself.

≈ 4 ≈
The Kundalini Shakti and Her Chakras

The Seven Chakras as Planes of Awareness

In the preceding pages of this book some mention has been made of the physical representation of the seven chakras in contrast to their spiritual significance. Either out of lack of qualification, as a ploy for making money, or a concession for beginners with animalistic tendencies who are still attached to the body, uninformed and unfaithful adherents of the Kundalini Yoga system have verily and purposefully reduced Her infinite scope — have "dumbed her down" to cater to the body and senses, what to speak of the ego.

But as the chart on the facing page demonstrates, and the quotes included in it proclaim, the system is a philosophy, and the philosophy is one of realization in positive action leading to blissful inaction and back. That is, as if attempting to constrict Kundalini Yoga to a physical method via physical means was not enough of a slam, the added insult of relegating her to the realm of bodily torsion, sweaty mats, and the excited pumping of the lungs to no spiritual avail, further lowers the ideal. To quote one well-known "teacher" of Kundalini Yoga, as stated in his own words, *"My classes for students begin with a*

The Seven Centers & Planes of Awareness & Existence

"Holding the highest note on the flute is very difficult. But one can come down and play with the other six notes of the instrument." Sri Ramakrishna Paramahamsa

↓ The Seven Centers of Awareness ↓

	The Seven Planes of Existence ↓	Special States of Higher Awareness

"WHEN THE KUNDALINI RISES TO THE SAHASRARA AND THE MIND GOES INTO SAMADHI, THE ASPIRANT LOSES ALL CONSCIOUSNESS OF THE OUTER WORLD. IN THAT STATE THE LIFE FORCE LINGERS FOR 21 DAYS AND THEN PASSES OUT. BUT IN THE CASE OF THE INCARNATIONS AND ISHVARAKOTIS THEY CAN DESCEND FROM THIS EXALTED STATE. THEY LIKE TO LIVE WITH THE DEVOTEES, ENJOY THE LOVE OF GOD, AND RETAIN A TRACE OF EGO SO THAT THEY CAN TEACH MEN. THEIR MINDS MOVE BETWEEN THE 6TH AND 7TH PLANES. THEY RUN A BOAT RACE, AS IT WERE, BETWEEN THESE TWO SUBTLE CENTERS."

7 — BRAHMALOKA

NIRVIKALPA SAMADHI

ASAMPRAJNATA SAMADHI

NIRVANA

TURIYA

SATORI

"THE 6TH PLANE CORRESPONDS TO THE AJNA CENTER. ITS PRESENCE IS AT THE EYEBROWS. IT HAS A LOTUS OF TWO PETALS. THERE ONE SEES THE FORM OF GOD. BUT THERE IS STILL A BARRIER. IT IS LIKE A LIGHT IN A LANTERN; YOU CANNOT TOUCH IT DUE TO THE GLASS."

6 — TAPARLOKA

BHAVAMUKHA

JADA SAMADHI

STHITA SAMADHI

"THE VISHUDDHA, THE 5TH PLANE, IS AT THE THROAT. IT HAS SIXTEEN PETALS. WHEN KUNDALINI REACHES IT, ONE WANTS TO TALK AND HEAR ONLY ABOUT GOD. TALK OF WORLDLY SUBJECTS CAUSE HIM PAIN."

5 — JANALOKA

SAVIKALPA SAMADHI

SAMPRAJNATA SAMADHI

CHETANA SAMADHI

"THE CENTER AT THE HEART CORRESPONDS TO THE 4TH PLANE OF THE VEDAS. IN THIS CENTER IS A LOTUS CALLED ANAHATA, WITH TWELVE PETALS."

4 — MAHARLOKA

SASMITA SAMADHI

BHAVA SAMADHI

"YOGA IS NOT POSSIBLE IF THE MIND DWELLS ON THE THREE LOWER PLANES OF EXISTENCE ONLY — THE MANIPURA, SVADHISTHANA, AND MULADHARA. A WORLDLY MAN'S MIND MOVES AMONG THESE THREE CENTERS, AT THE NAVEL, THE SEXUAL ORGAN, AND THE ORGAN OF EVACUATION. THESE THREE REPRESENT EATING, DRINKING, AND SEX LIFE. BUT WHEN KUNDALINI SHAKTI IS AWAKENED IT PASSES THROUGH THESE THREE LOWER CENTERS AND PIERCES THE HEART CHAKRA. THEN A MAN HEARS THE SUBTLE SOUND AND SEES LIGHT, AND HE CRIES OUT IN MUTE WONDER, 'OH! WHAT IS THIS! WHAT IS THIS!'"

3 — SVARLOKA

SANANDA SAMADHI

UNMANA SAMADHI

2 — BHUVARLOKA

NIRVICHARA SAMADHI

SAVICHARA SAMADHI

NIRVITARKA SAMADHI

1 — BHURLOKA

SAVITARKA SAMADHI

"KNOWN AS THE HELL REALMS, THE SEVEN PATALAS CORRESPOND GENERALLY TO THE SUBCONSCIOUS MIND OF HUMANITY WHEREIN ALL MANNER OF IRRATIONAL INSTINCTS, HABITS, IMPRESSIONS, AND MEMORIES ARE STORED. THESE RISE TO INFLUENCE THE THOUGHTS AND ACTIONS OF IGNORANT EMBODIED BEINGS WITHOUT THEIR BEING AWARE OF THE SOURCE OF THEM."

1. ATALA
2. VITALA
3. SUTALA
4. TALATALA
5. MAHATALA
6. RASATALA
7. PATALA

Kundalini Shakti Traversing the Seven Chakras

"With a magnifying glass one can make tiny objects look very big. Likewise, through the practice of Yoga one can detect the subtle spiritual lotuses." Mahendranath Gupta

Chart by Babaji Bob Kindler / Property of SRV Associations

fifteen minute warmup. Then a period of breathing exercises follow. After that, a half an hour of asana is given followed by five minutes of meditation, ending with the singing of a song." Five minutes of meditation? What benefit can possibly transpire in that meager amount of time? And where are the teachings? the scriptures? Mother Kundalini loves to rise in the sacred and powerful atmosphere of spiritual wisdom. As the great bhaktas of India sing, *"She does not accept cheap bribes."*

The purpose for any true spiritual practice is Self-realization — call it Enlightenment, Truth, or by any other contemporary term. If one reveres and follows the ancients, the fathers and mothers of these hoary systems, it is referred to as *samadhi, nirvana, turiya, satori* and a host of other names and descriptions, some of them placed in the left-hand column on the chart under scrutiny (page 41).

And what is being revealed is subtle, as evinced by Mahendranath Gupta's quote at the bottom of that chart. In it he likens the discovery of the chakras to subtle objects seen clearly only under a magnifying glass. And for the aspirant after Truth, this magnifying glass is his or her own awareness, polished and applied to such a refined and focused extent by yogic practice that the inner realms verily become open books for rapt study — living scriptures radiating and transmitting wisdom teachings spontaneously and continually. This is *Tattva Jnan,* communion with eternal principles, and it must be commingled with *Upasana Dhyan,* worshipful meditation upon the deities. This is Integral Yoga, again, called by many names.

The chart at hand (page 41) shows a series of quotes from Sri Ramakrishna Paramahamsa in direct conjunction with the names of the Seven Realms of Existence. The latter represent an ancient Vedic system which existed prior to the Vedantic age of the Upanisads. This great master has stated that the seven chakras of Kundalini Yoga coincide perfectly with these seven lokas of old India and her venerable *Rishis.*

At the bottom of this list are shown the seven *Patalas* as

well, the "sunken grounds" of base existence which correspond roughly with the concept of Christian hell. Descriptions of these are given in the secondary scriptures of India, and a version of them was also borrowed and re-proposed by the Buddhists later on. They are called such names as the "cracking freezing hell," and the "scalding burning hell," etc. There is, for instance, a hell for those miserly beings who, in their life or lives, kept all wealth for themselves and also kept others from having and enjoying it.

Whatever the case may be, and to escape the superstitious level of teaching which has come to inhabit the fundamentalist Christian idea that hell is an actual location in space and time, a much more enlightened interpretation renders these realms as the dream stuff of the mind where beings going to death with unresolved karmas and issues regress in order to get a good look at the errors of selfish existence and the transgressions they committed while on earth. In brief, these hells are a self-perpetrated and self-perpetuated conjuring of one's own conscience. Their real purpose is to effect the changing of the contents of the mind so as to better benefit the individual soul, thus all other beings. Interestingly enough, and much like the nectars and poisons inherent in the chakras, these seven patalas actually correspond to the seven higher worlds listed above them (that is, each higher world has its correlative companion or shadow), demonstrating once again the consistency of the principle of duality in all the worlds of form.

Sri Ramakrishna's words about the chakras (chart on page 41) are alive and inspirational. He presents them as inner realms rather than mere areas on the anatomical body. What is more, teachings attend every sentence. For instance, the observation that the three lowest chakras — Muladhara, Svadhisthana, and Manipura — correspond with the worldly acts of eating, drinking, and sex life of embodied beings on earth, draws an apt conclusion for seekers in general. And though it has been shown that these three chakras are foundational, and have their share of nectars to offer, they neverthe-less fulfill their highest purpose as doorways to the heart chakra, the Anahata.

The word "anahata," as has been mentioned, is another word for the sacred Om, such as *pranava, shabda,* etc. *"Oh! What is this? What is this?"* about says it all with regards to the only words a man can muster when *"awakened Kundalini passes through these three lower centers and pierces the heart chakra."* Otherwise, *"yoga is not possible if the mind dwells on the three lower planes of existence only."*

The philosophically informed student should be aware that the three planes of existence that correspond to these three foundational centers are noted as *Bhur, Bhuvah,* and *Svarlokas.* For anyone familiar with India's famous Gayatri mantra, the obvious fact comes to the fore that Bhur, Bhuvah, and Svaha are its first three words. In ancient Indian teach-ings, Bhurloka is the physical world, Bhuvarloka is the inter-mediary realm, and Svarloka corresponds to the heavens. Yes, they eat, drink, and have pleasurable relations in heaven too, which is also why they re-embody on earth after these desire-based experiences reach the end of a karmic cycle. Rebirth, or rounds of birth and death (in ignorance of one's Eternal Soul), what the Buddha called the *Kala-chakra,* is defined and brought forward for inspection here. The movement is com-posed of masses of beings and their unresolved karmas.

Life, "from the cradle to the grave," is not the only life, then, which is not necessarily good news — not for those who would, as Swami Vivekananda advises, transcend them both: *"This thirst for life, forever quench; it drags from birth to death and death to birth the soul."* The "soul," here, is the body/mind mechanism, ordinarily filled up with thought complexes and unfulfilled desires. The repetitive experience of birth and death, including what happens in-between, called convention-al life, is therefore suspect and, as the saying goes, pun intend-ed, "leaves a lot to be desired."

The realm of *Maharloka* is higher than heaven, where great seers keep their subtle bodies so as to work with the people of earth more readily. Just as earthly beings can occasionally feel and even commune with their ancestors in the Bhuvar and Svarlokas, so too can more advanced souls feel the presence of the saints and seers abiding at this higher level of existence. The corresponding chakra is the Anahata, or heart chakra. Great sense and reason come forth with such a wise association. It is as if real spiritual life begins when Kundalini Shakti decides to reside here. After gaining control of the prana via consciousness around food and action, the next real goal of the sadhaka of this system would be to penetrate the knot which separates the three lower chakras from this one at the heart. When perceived as an internal realm existing within one's own consciousness, all connections to what has been and what is to come — including the seamless tie to the Atman, the Indivisible Self — become more evident.

In some interpretations, the arrival of the soul at the Anahata chakra/Maharloka signals an end to the necessity for rebirth in the physical universe. Others opine that reaching Brahmaloka/Ajna chakra, only, puts an end to the tendency or habit of rebirth. Probably a good case could be made for the idea that the level of the center/realm that is reached is not the qualifying determinator, which lies instead within the quality or consistency of the soul. The Gods, even the saints and seers, are often seen to have a few desires left. Such beings may choose to come to earth to fulfill them, or in the case of greater luminaries, return to Bhurloka for the sake of freeing others. These are termed *Jivanmuktas* in Indian philosophy, or *Bodhisattvas* in Buddhism, whereas the *Videhamukta* — the one who has chosen to be free from all embodiment — "*has gone beyond, gone far beyond, to the Goal Supreme.*"

In any event, the next and radiant internal realm of *Janaloka* is mastered and traversed when Kundalini Shakti takes up Her auspicious residence in the *Vishuddha chakra* "at the throat." It is not hard to intuit this condition in another being, like in a sage or a spiritual preceptor, because the words which spill forth from the lips of such a being are all about God, Truth, and Wisdom, and are seldom about the world and its concerns. The famous story about Sri Ramakrishna tells of his finally becoming so weary of the talk of conventional people on worldly matters that he climbed the tower of the Kali temple one night and shouted out, *"Where are my loved ones, my disciples! My ears are being burned day and night with the talk of worldly people!"* Fortunately, and in a timely manner, his first students started arriving shortly thereafter. Janaloka, then, houses wisdom seers of a high caliber, the likes of Sanaka and Sanatkumar, for instance. These are very pure souls, as the name of the chakra relates — Vishuddha, "extremely pure."

But it is the "third eye" chakra which grabs the lion's share of attention in spiritual circles. It correlates with the *Taparloka*, an inner region of such rarefied atmosphere that the seven original Rishis of India, called the *Saptarishis*, are stationed there. The word, *"tapas,"* refers to the *"fire of yoga that burns away all dross from the gold of Consciousness."* It infers the ability to perform great austerities, the likes of which redeem whole worlds and countless striving and suffering souls.

The word, *"ajna,"* for which this center is named, is also of note. Jnana (jna) is wisdom of a specialized kind, associated specifically with spirituality and its concerns and attainments. Ajna indicates a level of awareness wherein wisdom is not needed, or, to put it in another way, where it has receded back into its own subtle cause. This would tend to describe the "third eye" region adequately, for as an earlier chart revealed for us, the nectars here broach closely, even intimately, upon the causal realm of Lord Brahma and the Trinity where the last vestiges of form are beginning to dissolve and fall away, revealing only the "Light of Absolute Consciousness."

To do justice to the Ajna chakra/Taparloka, the chart on the facing page (47) is offered up for scrutiny. Among other

Jnana Chakshu — The Wisdom Eye
Gross, Subtle, and Causal Sight

"The world is nothing but Brahman, because Brahman is the only Reality. See this always with your spiritual eye, and with an unruffled mind, and in all circumstances. For what is there to be seen here by the eye other than the mere objects of the senses? In like manner, to that one who knows Brahman, what is there to be seen at all — wherever the intellect may play — except Divine Reality?"
Shankara

1. Sees and utilizes the gross senses (*smelling, tasting, seeing, feeling, and hearing*)

2. Sees and utilizes the subtle senses (*odor, flavor, visibility, tangibility, audibility*)

3. Sees and utilizes the causal senses (*solidity, liquidity, luminosity, homogeneity, all-pervasiveness*)

Chart by
Babaji Bob Kindler

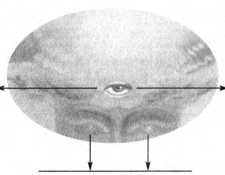

See only the objects of the senses

"The eyes are in the center of the forehead, but their gaze is always fixed on the three lower centers where eating, drinking, and sex-life are enjoyed." Sri Ramakrishna

1. *Avinashyantam*
Sees Reality as Imperishable.

2. *Sarvatra Samavathistam*
Sees Reality dwelling equally, everywhere.

3. *Prakrti Karma Kriyamanani*
Sees that nature performs all action, while the Soul, remains actionless.

Property of
SRV Associations

Religious References to the "Eye of Wisdom"

Christianity — *"If thine eye be single thou shalt know the Truth."* Jesus Christ

Hinduism — *"They who perceive with the eye of wisdom, they truly see. Devoting themselves to wisdom, they are neither born at the time of creation, nor are they disturbed at the time of dissolution. But the deluded do not see Me as I depart, stay, and enjoy. Only they truly see who possess the inner eye of wisdom."* Sri Krishna

Kundalini Yoga — *"As Kundalini traverses the sixth center, or 'Lotus,' called the Ajna Chakra, currents of refined prana rise high. Visions, light, and internal sounds are experienced, and the mind gets so absorbed that it loses normal consciousness."*

Buddhism — *"I have the true dharma hidden in my wisdom eye."* Sakyamuni Buddha

Taoism — *"The eyes are the windows of the soul. Between the two windows is the main door to divinity. Enter there to discover your inner divine nature."* Lao Tzu

Gnosticism — *"The True Gate is also the door to one's divine nature. It is the 'front door' to Heaven. It is located neither left nor right, up nor down. It is right in the center and thus is called the door to divinity — the White Sun."* Gnostic Mystic

Confucianism — *"Three persons are walking together; who is the master? They all have two eyes, but the divine Third Eye is the master of all of them."* Confucius

teachings it reveals the declarations of several different religions and lineages on the existence of the "third eye." In the *Bhagavad Gita*, Sri Krishna mentions the Ajna chakra. His statements to Arjuna on the battlefield at *Kurukshetra* are undeniable in this regard. For instance, speaking to the esteemed quality of *viveka*, discrimination between insentient Nature and the sentient Soul, between the changing and the Unchanging, He declared, *"They who perceive with the eye of wisdom this distinction between the field and its knower, and the deliverance of beings from this field of Prakriti, they go to the Supreme."* The eye of wisdom is therefore responsible for clear vision in the all-important area of spiritual discernment. Then, in an act demonstrating His Avataric nature, the illumined one touched Arjuna with His hand, saying:

na tu mam shakyase drastum anenai'va svachakshusa
divyam dadami te chaksuh pasya me yogam aisvaram

"But you cannot see Me with these ordinary eyes of yours;
Therefore I give you divine sight; behold My Supreme Yoga."

What followed is legend in scriptural history, left to all sincere seekers of Truth, whatever be their religion, to read and value.

The quote on this chart (page 47) is yet another example of Krishna's mention of the *Jnana Chakshu* in the Gita. But no less than the august religions of Christianity, Confucianism, Taoism, Buddhism, and Gnosticism speak out about this *"Doorway to Divinity,"* the *"White Sun,"* the *"Front Door to Heaven,"* and the *"Wisdom Eye."* In some esoteric Christian texts, the expression *"White Dove Descending"* is also found. Even, and maybe especially, among the Advaitists like Shankara, it is known as the *"Spiritual Eye."*

And in the Kundalini Yoga philosophy presently under study, this Ajna Chakra, or "two-petalled Lotus" at the third eye region, plays a significant role in the unfolding of full spiritual realization. Why should this be so? Despite the strange but intriguing disappearance of form when a man's consciousness rises to this center, the eye — even the physical eyes — are most wondrous in their abilities and capacities. If viewed from the singular standpoint of the inner analysis of one's own Consciousness, called *Atma Vichara*, the eyes are actually proof of the existence of the inner worlds spoken of herein.

The reasoning behind this is due to the fact that the human being sees without physical eyes. It is not blindness that is being spoken of here, although that is a case of special perception all its own. Rather, the existence of subtle worlds is proven by the repeated entrance of individual awareness into the dream state every night. Since a man sees in his dream state, he is availed of subtle senses, and these operate when the physical eyes are closed and abandoned by inner awareness.

The chart on page 47 illustrates this by citing the subtle senses, which are the power of the nose to perceive odor, the power of the tongue to taste, the power of the eyes to see, the power of the hands to feel, and the power of the ears to hear — i.e., odor, flavor, visibility, tangibility, and audibility. This "power" is not a physical property only, or even essentially. It originates from the mind's consciousness which, when traced to its ultimate Source, finds the Kundalini Shakti gazing back at it through the "Wisdom Eye." One might as well make a case for the existence of an "Inner Ear" as well, which hears in the dream state and detects the Primal Word, AUM, when entering into the ever-peaceful deep sleep state.

And there is no stopping here either. If one searches deeper, a causal world is perceived in which the eyes and their power to see, along with the ears and their power to hear, etc., have dissolved into the very idea of expression. As this chart relates, the primal concepts of solidity, liquidity, luminosity, homogeneity, and all-pervasiveness are the most subtle of the subtle, and the cause of everything which comes after them, sometimes and often inadequately referred to as "evolution."

• Yogic Connections and Correlations • in Meditation Practice

"Utilizing the supports (alambanas), the yogi stabilizes the mind-field by meditating upon them all, from the grossest magnitude inward to the subtlest principles. Let the yogi focus upon what is agreeable, then, observing it all in waking, dreaming, and deep sleep states with detachment.

— *Vedavyasa*

Alambanas, in Order of Meditation

Pancha Mahabhutas 5 Elements	Karmendriyas 5 Active Senses	Jnanendriyas 5 Cognitive Senses	Tanmatras 5 Subtle Elements	Mind/ Intellect

"Wisdom samadhi occurs via the process of gross thought to subtle thought, culminating in the indescribable state of 'I-am-ness.' In Abhava Yoga and Mahayoga, wherein one begins to see the blissful Self, the alambanas are absent. Thus, they are to be transcended in deep meditation."

Inward Connectivity in Meditation

Earth — Excreting — Smelling — Odor — Solidity

Water — Procreating — Tasting — Flavor — Liquidity

Fire — Locomotion — Seeing — Visibility — Luminosity

Air — Handling — Feeling — Tangibility — Homogeneity

Ether — Speaking — Hearing — Audibility — All-Pervasiveness

---

* The Three Origins *

Ahamkara, Ego ⟶ Buddhi, Determinative Intelligence ⟶ Mahat, Cosmic Mind

---

——— Meditate Upon Each Via ———

- its origin
- its qualities, attributes, characteristics
- its consistency and content
- its appearance in waking and dream
- its changing nature
- its place in the mind and thoughts
- its power and hold over the mind
- its disappearance in deep sleep

And so, mankind owns and operates — if he be aware, and if his Kundalini is awake, three sets of senses. The chart on the opposite page pursues this fact, replete with its yogic connections. What the sages and seers mean by the term, *"living in ignorance of one's true nature,"* is explained in this chart, having to do with connections — and disconnections. The complaint about modern man being divorced from nature, for instance, is not only a cause for concern on the environmental level, but more importantly, on primal and philosophical levels as well. The calamities and damages that mankind is wreaking upon nature would never have come about if he had always remained connected to nature as its master rather than becoming its slave. That is, though he might believe himself to be the master of nature, it is only from the standpoint of his ego that this is true. In reality, and until he has awakened to his true Nature, which is spiritual, he always remains in servitude to matter, when in actuality, all of nature has come out of him — out of his mind's vibrations. The word in Sanskrit, not found in English, is *Sankalpa*. It means "creative imaginings."

Here, on page 50, also reflected in the chart on page 47, we can see the same list of five causal elements/ideas listed under the mind/intellect column. If we follow them in reverse fashion, in order of cosmic appearance, we see that the idea of solidity in the mind gives birth to odor, which then transforms into the sense of smell, the power to excrete, all ending in the gross element, earth. To remove the "middle men," as they say, the idea of solidity in the Cosmic Mind (*Mahat, Pradhana, Hiranyagarbha, Lord Brahma*) is nothing other than the element earth, and therefore the planet earth.

The same applies for the other four sets of five. For instance (in coalescing the charts on pages 47 and 50), in the case of eyes, the subtle eyes, the causal eyes, and the 'Third Eye," the entire relationship is based upon the very idea, or cosmic concept, of luminosity. To explain further, when an unawakened man looks into the sky he sees the physical sun and, at best, only seeks to know it as a material entity. He eventually discovers that it is a ball of volatile fiery gases and rests easy with that knowledge. But when the illumined soul (one whose Kundalini has awakened) beholds the sun in the sky, he knows it to be only an outer manifestation of the very idea of light in the Mind of God — which is his own mind too, since he is spiritually awake. And what is more, that same light is known by the seer as the Light of Awareness — timeless, immutable, transformationless.

Therefore, a million suns in the nocturnal skies are no great cause of wonder for the seer, or for confusion or overwhelm for that matter. The entire panorama, *"this pictorial presentation before the mind and senses...." "....this fantasmagoria of fleeting phenomena,"* all lie within him. It is in this regard that the Upanisadic sage, about to give up the body in deepest meditation, declares to the Lord of the Universe: *"Like a lid, Thy shining golden orb covers the entrance to Truth. Therefore, remove Thyself, oh Sun, so that I who am devoted to the Truth may perceive It. Oh Sun, offspring of Prajapati, thou lonely courser of the heavens, controller and protector of all, contract Thy rays, withdraw thy external light so that I may behold that most blessed form of Light — my Self. I am indeed That One, that formless Being who enables the suns to shine, and who dwells in all."*

Returning to the problem of mankind's disconnection from nature, what the chart on page 50 is really proposing is a return to integrated life. This entails detecting and following a sort of "trail of breadcrumbs" by which modern man, if he is willing, can retrace ancient steps and obscure trails long overgrown to find what was lost over the long efflux of time. Of course, just "snapping to" and knowing the Self within would be the highest course, and most gratifying. But unfortunately for most beings there is still hell to pay on earth in the form of karmas from past lives. Thus, a gradual step-by-step process is advised wherein connections that are food for revelation, which is also the stuff of future realization, can be made.

In this method, which is in relation to Kundalini Yoga and its aims, the art of meditation is to be learned from a masterful soul. For it is only by developing the power to go inward that clear perception will return to the mind. The reclaiming of purified gross senses, subtle senses, and causal senses will be a directive that the seeker who desires healing must undertake and master. In Yoga, all the tattvas (the twenty-four principles of *Sankhya Yoga*) are to be inspected with these new sets of senses (subtle and causal). This will require taking up earth, water, fire, air, and ether, to begin, and meditating (not just studying them physically) upon them in several different modes. These are listed at the bottom of the chart presently under study (page 50) and will require apprenticeship of an illumined guru to allow hands-on experience and mastery.

This being accomplished, man — now a meditating thinker rather than a sense-bound animal — can be reconnected to the earth, and to all other principles which lie within himself. Following this course he may trace himself and the origins of all things to the Cosmic Mind and, "destroying" that (returning it to its cause), merge in AUM. This is classic involution of the spiritual variety, not restricted to mere planetary movements bound into cycles of physical evolution.

All of these aforementioned worlds and principles correlate with what Kundalini Yoga presents as chakras, spiritual vortexes of intelligent energy. As the chart on the next page illustrates, this yoga is not devoid of devotion and worship — another thing which it has been divested of by contemporary "teachers." The Kundalini Shakti is not just an energy, such as electric, kinetic, etc. She is the ever-conscious and Self-aware dynamic spiritual energy of pure Intelligence. She is an entity, as the meditating Yogis have found out, The Entity of their own inner terrain. This is why Sri Ramakrishna has stated that to attain liberation from the realms of name and form, one has to propitiate the *Mahashakti*, The Supreme Goddess. This is expressed most wonderfully via a poem from His Gospel.

The Kundalini Shakti and Her Chakras

Thou art the Primal Power, O Mother, She whose senses are controlled. The yogis meditate on Thee as Uma, great Himalaya's daughter. Thou who art the power of Siva, put to death my ceaseless cravings. Grant that I never fall again into the ocean of this world. Mother, Thou art the Primal Power, Thou, the five cosmic principles. Who can ever hope to know Thee, who art beyond all principles? Only for Thy bhaktas' sake dost Thou assume Thy various forms. But when Thy devotee's five senses merge in the five subtle elements, Mother, it is Thyself alone that he beholds as formless Truth.

Sahasrara Chakra
Symbol: Lotus
Petals: Thousand
Seed: None
Deity: Siva
Shakti: Kundalini

7

Highest of all, within the head, the soul-enthralling center is where shines the thousand-petalled lotus, Mahadeva's dwelling place. Having ascended to His Throne, O Spouse of Siva, sit beside Him!

> *"Whirlpools of dynamic energy which congeal the potent spiritual awareness of Kundalini Shakti, the chakras permeate the etheric, subtle, and causal bodies of mankind that are made up of unmanifested prakriti."*
> Babaji Bob Kindler

Ajna Chakra
Symbol: Triangle
Petals: Two Violet
Seed: Om
Deity: Siva/Shakti
Shakti: Hakini

6

And higher yet, between the eyebrows, blossoms the lotus of two petals, where the mind of man remains a prisoner and past controlling; from this flower one desires to watch the sportive play of life.

Vishuddha Chakra
Symbol: Silver Crescent
Petals: Sixteen Blue
Seed: Ham
Deity: Panchavakra Siva
Shakti: Shakini

5

Above, in the throat, is the sixteen-petalled lotus of smoky hue; there lies concealed a subtle space, transcending which one perceives the universe in space dissolve.

Anahata Chakra
Symbol: Circle
Petals: Twelve Green
Seed: Yam
Deity: Ishama Rudra
Shakti: Kakini

4

Beyond them lies the Lake of Nectar, in the region of the heart, where the twelve-petalled lotus flower enchants the eye with scarlet flame. When Thou dost open it, O Mother, touching it with Thy Lotus Feet, the age-long darkness of the heart instantly scatters at Thy sight.

Manipura Chakra
Symbol: Triangle
Petals: Ten Yellow
Seed: Ram
Deity: Rudra
Shakti: Lakini

3

At the navel is Manipura, the blue ten-petalled lotus flower; through the pathway of Sushumna Thou dost ascend and enter there. O Lady of the lotuses, in lotus blossoms Thou dost dwell.

Awakening

Longing

Svadhisthana Chakra
Symbol: Crescent Moon
Petals: Six Orange
Seed: Vam
Deity: Vishnu
Shakti: Rakini

2

Above it lies the Svadhisthana where the four-petalled lotus blooms. There also Thou dost make Thy home. O mystic power of Kundalini, in the four petals of that flower and in Vajrasana's six petals.

Muladhara Chakra
Symbol: Yellow Square
Petals: Four red
Seed: Lam
Deity: Brahma
Shakti: Dakini

1

Knowledge

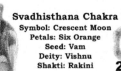

Mother, in every living creature Thou dost have Thy dwelling-place. As Kundalini Thou dost live in the Lotus of the Muladhara.

Worship

Thy Name, I have heard, O Consort of Siva, is the destroyer of our fear. And so on Thee I cast my burden; Save me, O kindly Mother. Out of Thy Womb the world is born, and Thou it is who dost pervade it. Art thou Kali? Art Thou Radha? Who can rightly say?

Chart by Babaji Bob Kindler

Property of SRV Association

Beginning at the bottom of the chart on the facing page, the aforementioned poem/song (also listed on page 261 of the *Gospel of Sri Ramakrishna*), a favorite of the Great Master, both describes Mother Kundalini as the illumined souls have found Her, and traces Her inward course amidst the seven chakras which are Her congealing points along this most auspicious spiritual journey. All of the specialized qualities which emanate from those of enlightened mind and character — what is often called the "Rain cloud of Virtues" — and all other attributes, boons, blessings, and spiritual experiences, spring from Her by the grace of Her Divine Will. Thus, She is the most beloved of the most percipient of devotees, whether they prefer form or formless Reality.

The image on this chart shows and describes Her, not only as the spiritual power that is coursing through the gross, subtle, and causal bodies of the devotees, but also as the one who is worshipping and showing the way of Kundalini Shakti — the path to Lord Siva, the Paramasiva. The Mother in human form, attended by the most auspicious presence of Her dutiful son, Sri Ganesha, participates in formal worship of Lord Siva, offering Him flower garlands, sandalpaste, kum-kum, sanctified fruits, sweets, and curd — all with the most ardent and intense devotion combined with mantras and utterances of devotional song. The devotee, gazing upon this awesome and heartening spectacle, can but only do the same, breaking into spontaneous praises of Her, and Him, in poetic and musical forms:

> *Thy Name, I have heard, O Consort of Siva,*
> *is the destroyer of our fear.*
> *And so upon Thee I cast my burden;*
> *Save me, O kindly Mother.*
> *Out of Thy Womb the world is born,*
> *and Thou it is who dost pervade it.*
> *Art Thou Kali? Art Thou Radha? Who can rightly say?*

Mother, in every living creature Thou dost have Thy dwelling-place.
As Kundalini Thou dost live in the Lotus of the Muladhara.
Above it lies the Svadhisthana where the four-petalled lotus blooms.
There also Thou dost make Thy home, O mystic power
of Kundalini, in the four petals of that flower
and in Vajrasana's six petals.

At the navel is Manipura, the blue ten-petalled lotus flower;
through the pathway of Sushumna Thou dost ascend and enter there.
O Lady of the lotuses, in lotus blossoms Thou dost dwell.
Beyond them lies the Lake of Nectar, in the region of the heart,
where the twelve-petalled lotus enchants the eye with scarlet flame.
When Thou dost open it, Mother, touching it with Thy Lotus Feet,
the age-long darkness of the heart instantly scatters at Thy sight.

Above, in the throat, is the sixteen-petalled lotus of smoky hue;
there lies concealed a subtle space, transcending which
one perceives the universe in space dissolve.
And higher yet, between the brows, blossoms the lotus of two petals,
where the mind of man remains a prisoner and past controlling;
from this flower one desires to watch the sportive play of life.

Highest of all, within the head, the soul-enthralling center
is where shines the thousand-petalled lotus,
Mahadeva's dwelling place.
Having ascended to His Throne, O Spouse of Siva,
sit beside Him!

Thou art the Primal Power, O Mother,
She whose senses are controlled.
The yogis meditate on Thee as Uma, great Himalaya's daughter.
Thou who art the power of Siva,
put to death my ceaseless cravings.
Grant that I never fall again into the ocean of this world.

Mother, Thou art the Primal Power,
Thou, the five cosmic principles.
Who can ever hope to know Thee, who art beyond all principles?
Only for Thy bhaktas' sake dost Thou assume Thy various forms.
But when Thy devotee's five senses merge
in the five subtle elements, Mother,
it is Thyself alone that he beholds as formless Truth.

Each chakra, as this chart (page 54) reveals, possesses a particular color, an inherent seed sound (bijam), an indwelling deity, and an aspect of shakti all its own. The number of petals also changes with each, signifying the number of nadis, or subtle nerves, which lead to and away (beyond) from it. When adept yogis or yoginis attain purification of body, senses, and mind, they develop certain abilities, spiritually speaking, which qualify them for perceiving higher realms of Awareness and the experiences specific to those dimensions. As Sri Ramakrishna and others have said, this is a very personal and mystical inner process. It must be experienced in order that full comprehension of it dawn. Mere words, no matter how beautiful, will never do it complete justice.

In addition to all of this, the poem mentions outright several of the principles cited earlier in this book, and held as axioms in the different darshanas of India — like the five senses, the five elements, and the five subtle elements. The dissolution of the realms of name and form as indicated by the Samadhi of Vedanta and the Nirvana of Buddhism, also receives attention. Thus does the noble system of Kundalini Yoga both affirm India's Religion and Philosophy overall, and contribute fresh and experientially-based wisdom to them as well, leaving us with a deep-seated and impelling desire to know all aspects of our being, especially those most sacrosanct twin roots of living, breathing, humanity — the Archetypical Couple called Shiva and Shakti.

≈ 5 ≈

Tantra's Shiva and Shakti

The Archetypical Couple's Perfect Relationship

The real and final purpose of Kundalini Yoga is the uniting of the Mahashakti with Paramashiva at the "crown of the head," the seventh chakra, or *"lotus of a thousand petals,"* called the *Sahasrara*. The coursing upwards, inwards, of Kundalini force is at the behest of a consummate urge for the reuniting of Shiva and Shakti principles, or as Truth seekers would call it, a supreme and pure desire for ultimate freedom. Special tantric words of great significance such as *vichikirsha* (a divine desire for union and infinite expansion), and *svatantriya* (a state of absolute independence), come to mind and apply here. All that is *mangalam*, auspicious — good and beyond good — originate in Them and flow forth from Them as well.

The offering of another chart, on the facing page, shares some valuable teachings on Shiva and Shakti given by the experts of Tantra science and philosophy. These are revealed for all to see and study. Certain of these, however, require some commentary which will expand the knowledge base of those who are specifically interested in this otherwise esoteric and recondite system of spirituality, and which will aid the practitioner in the internal act of meditation so crucial to the consummation of its aims.

Tantra's Shiva & Shakti

"Shaktayika, dynamic power, and Agama, knowledge of the use of that power, are identical with one another. Thus, Shiva is the agent, and Shakti, the instrument. But Shakti's manifestations are, in essence, Shiva appearing as the imminent — all life in the worlds of name and form."

Tantra Darshana

- Siva is synonymous with Brahman, and represents Kula the aspiring family guided by live spiritual tradition.

- Siva is Niskala, the subtle backdrop underlying all.

- Siva is Tat, "That Alone," and Purnahanta, "I in Fullness" — which is Siva in tandem with His unstinted freedom as Shakti.

- Siva is the indeterminate state (alinga) from which arises all vibrations (spandas), which then manifest as principles (tattvas) amidst which Shakti sports in time (kala) as the play of Consciousness.

Siva

- Siva is also the determinative state (linga), who in conjunction with nature, is called Sakala Siva.

- Siva's essential functions are projection (sristhi), sustenance (sthiti), dissolution (samhara), self-limitation (tirodhana), and expression (anugraha).

- Siva wields His two main consciousness forces, called the Parigraha Shaktis (Bindu and Maya), which both cause and oversee all worlds and forms in space and time.

- The Bindu and Maya Shaktis fulfill Siva's Four Great Works: Jnana pada, maintaining philosophical systems; Yoga pada, spiritual disciplines; Charya pada, teaching; Kriya pada, fructification.

Shakti

- Shakti is the form of Siva: Sivarupah. Thus, worship of Shakti is the stepping-stone to both the destruction of ignorance and the attainment of freedom.

- Shakti is directly correlative to Guru Tattva, via which the spiritual preceptor appears and spiritual teachings are duly transmitted.

- Shakti and Her worship accomplishes the full involution of the embodied soul back to the Source by withdrawing the Atman from Its many associations with Her mayic creations.

- Invoking Shakti awakens the Kundalini power lying dormant in all living beings.

- Propitiating Shakti reveals the Atman to be pure and sentient, and all manifest principles (tattvas) to be pure and insentient.

"Shiva and Shakti are pure Existence combined with inner Essence. Existence precedes Essence, but Essence renders Existence meaningful. Siva and Shakti's innate inseparability is the root of all expression. As long as beings do not realize it they move about in a confusing haze of illusory phenomena, devoid of the real import of humanity's relationship with God and with each other." Tantra Darshana

Two of these teachings are particularly supportive of living beings who may not, as yet, have developed spiritual abilities to any great extent. The fact that Lord Shiva represents *Kula*, the ideal dharmic family, and radiates as well as *Sakala*, Consciousness in Nature, inspires the Godward-moving people of this world to emulate Him in all ways. As Sri Ramakrishna has said about this world, *"Everywhere I look I see nothing but the union of Shiva and Shakti."* This is a way of seeing God in everything, just short of but related to the more extreme and difficult vision of perceiving the Formless Brahman.

And as the chart relates, Shiva is underlying this world of name and form. A more tangible and tactile way of perceiving Him is through the existence of His Shakti and Her powers. However, if beings devoid of knowledge and faith look out through the senses connected to the mind they may see only maya — confusing, and beguiling, albeit insentient. But one who has awakened spiritually, or, as we say in Kundalini Yoga speak, has straightened his coil and lit up the chakras with the Light of Awareness (Kundalini Shakti), beholds the workings of the Mahashakti in everything, everywhere.

Tantra calls this power *shaktayika*. It takes knowledge to direct Her, for She is only physical energy and life force to the unawakened. But Shiva knows Her as pure Awareness. To Him She is also *Parigraha Shakti*, representing twin forces of Consciousness. They aid Him with His five essential functions which He utilizes to sustain four great works. In other words, the Benign Shiva projects, sustains, and dissolves the worlds of name and form, and also instills them with their limitations and various modes of expression. When the embodied soul is ready for deeper realization, these limitations get lifted by degrees and the modes of expression grow more divine.

All the while, the four great works are sustained — *Jnana pada*, *Yoga pada*, *Charya pada*, and *Kriya pada*. Books such as this one are products of *Jnana pada*, the maintenance over ages of eternal spiritual philosophies and their principles and teachings. By the longevity of such systems, the wise, from lifetime to lifetime, from age to age (*yuge yuge cha dharmasya*), can look back into the wisdom of the seers for clues on how to help humanity to attain the Ultimate Goal. This wisdom is *Shruti*, those scriptures that declare the nondual Truth in no uncertain terms, free of any obfuscation or overlays. There is also what is called *Smriti*, testaments which reveal to the seeker how to live a dharmic life free of maya and its adverse effects. The existence, even survival, of religion and philosophy — married to and never divorced from one another — is one of the supreme works of Lord Shiva.

The principle of *Yoga pada* comes next. There must always be in effect and existence a few cross sections of humanity given to the study of these aforementioned works, and more importantly, the actual practice and inculcation of their teachings. This way, both a precedent and standard around sadhana can be set and established, and a cogent telling of the further experiences of the sages and seers in the infinite firmament of spirituality can be recorded and sustained.

And it is out of this august institution that *Charya pada* finds it material. There must be teachers, gurus, acharyas, or spiritual preceptors to both spread the message of Truth in the world and transmit it locally among any given group of spiritual adherents who crop up around them. The most exemplary of these entourages are the direct disciples, apostles, and followers of the Avatars of the world — Buddha's noble eight, Christ's twelve apostles, Shankara's group of monastic and lay disciples and, in more recent times, Sri Ramakrishna's sixteen *sannyasins*. In a contemporary but imbalanced world of violence and revenge that has given birth to such abominations as "terrorist cells," these above-mentioned groups represent "peace cells." These encourage the spread of wisdom which will quell the unruly passions of inflamed minds, bringing the light of reason and the presence of God into otherwise tenebrous human hearts and minds.

Kriya pada is the fourth of Lord Shiva's great works. In this context it is the fructification of selfless works which is inferred. It is not the expectations of fruits which come about in cause and effect manner via the ongoing world processes, but rather that divinely willed spontaneous manifestation of fruits unasked for and unsought. This is a boon from Shiva, fully matured and perfectly timed so as to allow no deviation or impedance in either earthly life or spiritual experience. And in fact, all transgressions are effectively neutralized there, and blessings for future realizations are contained therein.

The chart on the facing page shows the four padas of Siva and His two Parigraha Shaktis. Some classic Tantric ideology about His five essential functions should also be given.

Students of Tantric philosophy, as well as of Yoga and Vedanta, are aware of Siva's crucial role as "destroyer" among the Hindu Trinity, alongside of Brahma and Vishnu. As Paramasiva in Shaivism, He stands alone (as Mahavishnu does in Vaishnavism) as the holder of all three functions Himself. These three, usually translated as "creation, preservation, and destruction," are herein called "projection, sustenance, and dissolution" and comprise three of Siva's five essential functions. The reason to change the old designation to the newer one is simply put: creation out of nothing, as Western Theology sees it, is not sensible. The entire manifestation is a mental projection from the Cosmic Mind, or Siva in this case. Destruction, too, is not possible; for everything, sentient and insentient, merely goes into abeyance in Unmanifested Prakriti at the end of a cycle and rests there until it is time for a new cycle to begin. Then it is projected forth once again.

As for His other two essential functions — *Tirodhana* and *Anugraha* — the chart defines them as Self-Limitation and Self-Expression. By the term Self-Limitation is meant that all of the shortcomings, imperfections, inadequacies, inefficiencies — even errors and transgressions — are placed into the Cosmic plan by Lord Siva Himself, and he lifts and does away

Siva's Two Shaktis, Four Padas, & Five Functions

"The relation between Siva and Shakti goes beyond all types of characterizations. It is a mystery realizable in the light of Self-expression as Consciousness."
Manoranjan Basu

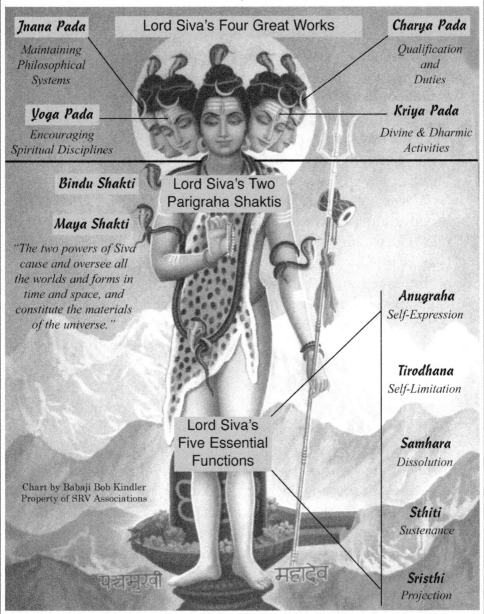

Jnana Pada
Maintaining Philosophical Systems

Lord Siva's Four Great Works

Charya Pada
Qualification and Duties

Yoga Pada
Encouraging Spiritual Disciplines

Kriya Pada
Divine & Dharmic Activities

Bindu Shakti

Maya Shakti

Lord Siva's Two Parigraha Shaktis

"The two powers of Siva cause and oversee all the worlds and forms in time and space, and constitute the materials of the universe."

Anugraha
Self-Expression

Tirodhana
Self-Limitation

Samhara
Dissolution

Lord Siva's Five Essential Functions

Chart by Babaji Bob Kindler
Property of SRV Associations

Sthiti
Sustenance

Sristhi
Projection

"Shiva has five functions to perform through His Shaktis. He is Satya-sankalpa and Apta-kama — His resolves are all true and His desires are eternally accomplished. He makes the world evolve so that individual souls can be released through the removal of their impurities." Manoranjan Basu

with them when the time is right. Thus, the entrance of consciousness into limited forms is really an act of Siva, and the veils, karmas, and other many obscurations which beings labor under are dissolved as they draw nearer to Him over the span of their lifetimes. Anugraha, Self-Expression, concerns both the fulfillment of desires for purification of the Jivas, and the manifestation of God in form for the sake of sportive play. The Divine thus becomes the eternal companion of all aspiring souls, and all suffering ones as well. What gets expressed in these relationships is love of God — which is its own fruit.

The dynamic power of Shakti is nothing other than Shiva in manifestation, and the presence of Shiva is nothing less than Shakti as underlying intelligence. Their relationship is perfection. As the Tantras teach, *"Siva is the indeterminate state from which arises all vibrations, amidst which Shakti sports in time as the play of Consciousness."* Thus, Shakti is the real form of Shiva, ensuring that all ignorance gets destroyed and that beings remember their inherent freedom and return to it after expressing themselves in the embodied state. To quote the Tantras again, *"Shakti and Her worship accomplishes the full involution of the embodied soul back to the Source by withdrawing the Atman from its many associations with Her mayic creations."*

Shakti and Her worship are certainly nothing to be overlooked or underestimated. She is not a matter for mere ritualism either. Bowing and offering flowers in the temple are mere nothings without seeing Her first and foremost abiding in the shrine of the human heart — and serving Her there. As the Tantras say, *"You are the darling of your own worship."* Thus, Shakti's intention is to awaken the Kundalini power lying dormant in potential aspirants. She states, *"As long as beings do not realize their inner nature, they only move about in a confusing haze of illusory phenomena, devoid of the real import of humanity's relationship with God and with each other."* Perhaps it is time for humanity to meditate on the Goddess, then, and awaken Her superlative Kundalini power within them.

≈ 6 ≈

The Devi Gita

Meditation on the Goddess

One of the fine appeals of the Kundalini Yoga philosophy is its congeniality with the paths of form and formlessness both. Whereas the seeker and practitioner can certainly take up an image of the Goddess and envision Her within as guide and companion, it is extremely difficult to pin Her down to a specific form. That is, when the Kundalini force is alive and flowing through the nadis and spiritual centers, She seems entirely formless, a fact that endears Her and Her system to jnanis and nondualists, as well as to karmis and bhaktas.

Whatever the type of one's temperament, the simple fact remains that, as some have said, the many pass while the One remains the same. The wise thus learn to focus on this immutable Presence, so easily accepted as Mother, and render all other considerations subservient to Her. Besides, other than being subtle and formless, She is also extremely personable. She graces even the gods with pertinent instruction, appearing to them when She is most needed. In scriptures like the *Devi Mahatmyam* and the *Srimad Devi Bhagavatam*, She appears to them most often on the battlefield, when circumstances are dire. Since She is the imminent power in everything — from energy in food, to the life force in the elements, body, and senses, and inward to the very force of Kundalini Shakti — Her instructions are both honest and effective.

Meditation on the Goddess

The "Devi Gita" from the Srimad Devi Bhagavatam

"Throughout life, everything is to be done in the light of My Great Hrillekah mantra, whose gifts are the guru and all the blessings which naturally come to My devotees. Nothing at all, at any time, is unattainable to the one who worships the Devi."

"Meditate on My Thousand-petaled Lotus."

"Perform all actions in the light of the great Devi Mantra."

"Remember and envision your blessed guru."

"Perceive youth, the aged, the poor, and the public, all as forms of Me."

"Meditate on My form in the fire of Kundalini in the Muladhara."

"Feed the holy, the hungry, and the devotees."

"Contemplate the Hrillekah mantra in tandem with the chakras."

"Dance joyfully and sing My Names."

"Ruminate on the four boons."

"Recite My many names and read My Upanisads."

"Meditate on the five seats of the Devi, all situated under My Lotus Feet."

"Make offerings to all the deities in My sacred Mandala."

"Perform puja for Me with devotion, and with all sacred offerings."

"Perform concentrated Japa and offer the results to Me, the Devi."

The Five Seats of The Devi

Brahma

Ishvara

Vishnu

Sadasiva

Siva

Chart by Babaji Bob Kindler

And Her instructions are verily scripture. Therefore, Her dearest and deepest children both know and love Her. They worship Her but also study Her word in the shastras. For the seers, saints, and sages are Her select children sent to earth to maintain and transmit Her wisdom as saving grace. As one beautiful song of India states, *"Oh Mother, the six darshanas are powerless to reveal You. Indeed, You reveal them."* The six darshanas are the definitive spiritual views of Mother India which developed throughout time — essential philosophies such as Yoga, Sankhya, and Vedanta. Thus, there is a very good reason why scriptures such as the *Yoga Kundalini Upanisad* equate Kundalini Shakti with *Sarasvati*. Sarasvati is reverently called the *Vak Devi*, or "Mother of the Word." She is the teacher of Wisdom, especially of the spiritual variety called *Paravidya*. Thus, those who love Her want to know Her, and do so by consulting, studying, and memorizing the scriptures.

On the facing page is seen a condensation into chart form of the *Devi Gita* found in the *Srimad Devi Bhagavatam*. This is Her own song of purifying and strengthening teachings. A new English translation is given following this chapter to conclude this book, and as a gift for all who would propitiate Her as the Highest Ideal.

Beginning at the top middle of this chart and proceeding clockwise by following the arrows, the spiritual aspirant can trace the vein of Her instruction to effect a daily sadhana that is both well-guided and conducive of full realization. As She says herein, *"There is nothing at all, at any time, which is unattainable to the one who worships Me."* Before this worshipful meditation begins, however, a look at a few of Her foundational teachings will prepare the aspirant for the fullest measure of spiritual gain in the process.

The Divine Mother of the Universe, also known as the Kundalini Shakti, the *Adyashakti, Mahavidya Mahamaya,* and other superlative names and appellations, is that formless form Who informs the mind and all the worlds with Her various modes and levels of energy. In Her most superlative scripture, the *Srimad Devi Bhagavatam*, She discourses to the gods, seers, and devotees on Her Kundalini Yoga system and its directive of flooding the spiritual centers with Her Light. This is esoteric wisdom to be sure, mystical in nature, and fully capable of ushering in that most sublime expression known as "spiritual experience," which is extremely rare in the world, and in embodied beings. In Her own words, She states:

"There are some 350,000 nadis in the triple body of man; of these, there are ten principle ones. Out of these ten there are three primary. The foremost of these three is the Sushumna, of the nature of moon, sun, and fire, to be envisioned in the center of the spinal cord. To the left of that is the Ida, white, shining with the luster of the moon. Its nature is primeval force, feminine, and it is nectar-like. On the right of the Sushumna is the Pingala, luminous like the sun, and of the nature of the masculine mode.

"In the inmost and deepest part of the Sushumna canal there exists a triple aspect of Shakti, abiding in the form of a subtle web. These three aspects are My will (Iccha Shakti), My wisdom (Jnana Shakti), and My ability of spontaneous action (Kriya Shakti). Above them floats My bijam, Hrim. Hovering over all of these is the serpent fire itself, called Kula Kundalini — red, inflamed, always intoxicated. Around Her is the subtle chakra, Adhara, yellow in color. The yogis meditate on this. In its center is a hexagonal space wherein resides the Muladhara Chakra. It is the pitham, the base of all the other chakras which stretch within and above.

"Next is encountered the Svadhisthana, sporting six petals with six letters. It emits a diamond-like luster. Its root syllable, 'sva,' refers to the Param Linga of Lord Siva, so the sages call it Svadhisthana.

"Deeper, and next in line, is the Manipura Chakra, looking like lightning in clouds, sporting ten petals designating ten letters. Appearing as a giant pearl, it thus gets its name of 'Manipura.' Vishnu dwells there, so meditating upon that chakra elicits an auspicious vision of Him.

"Coursing inwards, the next arrival place for my subtle force of dynamic power is the Anahata Chakra, with twelve petals and twelve letters. Centered in this chakra is what is called the Banalingam, resplendent like the sun. This lotus emits the primal Word known to the yogis as 'Shabda Brahman,' even without being struck or initiated whatsoever. It is a source of never-ending joy. Rudra, the Highest Person, dwells there.

"Deeper, higher, there is the Vishuddha Chakra of sixteen petals and sixteen letters. It is of a smoky color but very radiant. Its physical correlation is with the throat, where wisdom words ushering in beatific visions are uttered. Here, the Jivatman perceives the Paramatman and is forever purified. This chakra is also known as the 'Akasha Chakra.'

"Next, and infinitely inwards, is seen the Ajna Chakra, its outer correlation being with the 'third eye' seated in the center of the forehead, between the eyebrows. It has two petals sporting the seed syllables 'Ha' and 'Ksa.' The true Self of mankind resides in this lotus. When Consciousness is stationed here it becomes all-seeing, all-knowing — always fully aware of past, present, and future. Commands from the Highest Deity come from here.

"The center beyond all centers resides above that, beyond the minor chakras of Kailasa and Rodhini. It is the Vindusthan, or Sahasrara of a thousand petals — indescribable. Arriving there the aspirant has successfully followed the highest path to Yoga.

"Thus I have described the Adhara Chakras and some of their qualities. The seeker after freedom is first to consider and then render sacred all acts and deeds. Then, by pranayam, he is to fix the mind on the Muladhara and arouse the Kula Kundalini power there. Piercing then, in order as described, all the aforementioned chakras, he is to transfer that power inwards to the heart, then unite Me with Siva at the crown of the head. When this is accomplished there is produced a kind of red nectar, intoxicating, and the yogi is to make an offering of that to the Maya Shakti and all the deities residing in the various lotuses. When this act is accomplished all are pleased, and one can efficiently return to the Muladhara region."

Mother Kali — The Adyashakti

Chart by Babaji Bob Kindler   Property of SRV Associations

> Worship of Kali, called Brahmakalarupah >

Shakti Jnanam Vina Devi Nirvana Naiva Jayate

"There can be no liberation without knowledge of the Wisdom Mother."

ॐ ऐं ह्रीं

> Worship of Lesser Deities >

Kaivalya Nirvana Mukti

Gauna Mukti

Ekananda Chidakritih

Eka = Single principle
Ananda = Complete contentment
Chid = Consciousness / Intelligence
Akritih = Essential Nature

Dharana Yoga	Avyaya Yoga
1) Focus mind to balance the breath	1) Fix attention upon Mother's Feet
2) Fix mind on the Muladhara Chakra	2) Fix attention on Mother's Hands
3) Arouse the Kundalini Shakti	3) Fix attention on each of Her limbs
4) Pierce each ascending Chakra	4) Practice until the heart gets pure
5) Carry shakti energy upwards	5) Fix your heart on Her full Form
6) Settle in the Sahasrara Chakra	6) Practice japa of Her mantra
7) Meditate on Shiva & Shakti there	7) Meditate on Her mantra as Her
8) Gather nectar from Their union	8) Transform Brahman into Knowledge
9) Offer it lovingly to the Maya-shakti	9) Fuse mantra practice with Yoga
10) Offer some to all the lower Deities	10) Dissolve the mind into Her
11) Descend to the Muladhara Chakra	
12) All mantras will now yield success	

"By practice of Dharana Yoga one will become free of this Samsara filled with old age and death. Dharana Yoga means to fix one's heart and mind fully on the supremely lustrous Form of Mine which pervades all the quarters, worlds, and countries. I am the World Mother. My devotees will get all of My qualities; there is no doubt of this. This Yoga leads to the knowledge of the union between the Jiva and Brahman."

"Avyaya Yoga prescribes practice of mantra combined with yogic prowess. First, receive instructions from a Guru. Millions of books will not give you realization, but time spent with the Guru will confer It. By meditating on the mantra, the thing to be known, called Brahman, gets transformed into Knowledge. The mantra is futile without Yoga; Yoga is futile without the mantra. Together they are an infallible means to realize Brahman. The Jivatman, made invisible by Maya, is seen as identical with Paramatman via the mantra."

"Among castes, Brahmins are foremost; among sadhikas, shaktas are foremost; and among the foremost of the shaktas are the worshipers of Kali."   Srimad Devi Bhagavatam

The Divine Mother of the Universe prescribes other preparatory forms of practice as well, called *Dharana* and *Avyaya Yogas*. On the facing page is a breakdown of the specific practices that these yogas entail, along with some other salient teachings. The aspirant should practice these, one or the other, according to qualification, instructed by one's spiritual guide. In the scriptures, the Goddess states the following about these two yogas, both being a further condensation of the Kundalini process itself:

"Now hear from Me about Dharana Yoga. To fix thoroughly one's heart and mind upon the supremely lustrous Form of Mine, pervading all quarters and all countries, soon leads to the union of the Jiva and Brahman.

"If one cannot adequately effect this with any speed owing to the impurities of the heart, then he must adopt what is called Avyaya Yoga. In this effort, the sadhaka should fix the heart and mind on My gentle Feet, Hands, Limbs, and Form in succession, and try to fix his inner vision on each of these in turn and together. The mind will become pure in this practice, and with that pure mind he can soon envision My entire Form in meditation.

"From here, the devotee is to practice the Mantra via Japam and Homam until the mind gets dissolved into My Consciousness. By the practice of meditating on the Mantra, the thing to be known, Brahman gets transformed into wisdom. Know for certain that the Mantra is futile without Yoga, and that Yoga is futile without the Mantra. Together they are the two infallible means by which to realize Brahman. As the jar in a dark room is visible by the light of a lamp, so too is the Jivatman, surrounded by the darkness of Maya, made visible by means of My Mantra repeated in deference to and in honor of the Highest Paramatma.

"These are the subsidiary Yogas and their angas (limbs). I have described them for your own highest good. You should receive instructions about them from the mouth of your guru, else millions of Shastras (scriptures) will never be able to give you true realization of the meanings of these Yogas."

Referring back to the chart on page 66, *Meditation on the Goddess*, we find that there is a profound import placed upon the mantra, especially Mother mantra in the form of the *Hrillekah Mantra* (see page 80). Those who receive the mantra in this lifetime are extremely fortunate, as are those who are, to quote Sri Krishna in the *Bhagavad Gita*, "*...following the thread of their yoga from a past lifetime.*" Those who do not receive the mantra from an authentic preceptor are as yet unqualified to do so. Those who receive it but do not practice it, or who give up the practice before it has matured or, worst of all, who betray the Guru's sacred trust, are as "thieves in the night." In these latter at least a seed has been planted, and another chance at Self-realization will arise in a future lifetime.

On the chart under study (page 66), the lower portion displays the Five Seats of the Devi — *Brahma, Vishnu, Siva, Ishvara,* and *Sadasiva.* They are all Her representatives on the earth plane, as well as being openings to higher Consciousness. In the scriptures, The Devi states:

"*Brahma, Vishnu, Rudra, Ishvara, and Sadasiva are my Divine Regents. They are the presiding deities of earth, water, fire, air, and akasha respectively. No one will see the Goddess without first perceiving them. It would be easier for a man to capture the elements and the akasha as if they were an antelope skin than to root out and destroy all the miseries of this world without first knowing these five deities and the Goddess. In other words, it is impossible. Therefore, My Svetashvatara Upanisad states that 'Those who are engaged in deepest meditation, only they see through the tamas, rajas, and sattva of the forms incarnated respectively of these five great deities.'*"

Meditation on the Goddess as advised by Her is shown in clockwise order on the chart on page 66. The sincere aspirant whose love for the Goddess is pure and constant will ardently follow this guided contemplation inside the mind every morning, enjoying and benefitting by its results. The proper order, given next with commentary, is as follows:

1) "Remember and envision the blessed Guru."

Spiritual life is always attended by the spiritual guide. Those who are without a guru are as yet still seeking such a boon. They may be unprepared for such an advent, or still dabbling in spiritual pursuits via recourse to a host of teachers on the surface level. When the true guru, called the *Mantri Guru*, is found, the mantra is transmitted in sacred ceremony and authentic spiritual life begins. The guru will be there eternally for reference and guidance. Thus, remembering that divine personage daily brings auspiciousness to one's self-efforts. This consists of envisioning the form of one's guru in the heart, in company with the Chosen Ideal (Ishtam) to whom the mantra the guru has duly transmitted correlates. Envisioning and saluting the preceptor is thus a part of the seeker's everyday ritual.

2) "Meditate on My Form in the Fire of Kundalini in the Muladhara."

This Fire was discussed on page 68 in accordance with the Muladhara Chakra and its exploration and penetration. It is primal, intense, and can be looked at as the initial entrance into one's higher Awareness — an appropriate atmosphere in which to begin the act of "straightening one's coil." A goodly amount of time each day can be spent basking in and realizing the import of this unique, purifying spirit. Thus, different forms of Agni, the deity of fire, are utilized as aids in sadhana.

3) "Contemplate My Hrillekah Mantra in tandem with the chakras."

Receiving the Mother mantra from the guru, the practice of japa ensues based upon knowing what all the matras (letters) of the mantra signify. This knowledge, combined with meditation, will help unlock the doors to the various lotuses. In this way the mantra acts as a password, or key, that allows one freer access to the internal realms of Consciousness.

4) "Ruminate on the Four Boons."

The four boons are: *Dharma* (righteousness/divine life), *Jnana* (wisdom), *Vairagyam* (detachment), and *Lakshmi* (prosperity). It is good to meditate on the opposites of these qualities as well (unrighteousness, attachment, ignorance, and lack of wealth) so that the nature of ordinary mind, which is dual, can be comprehended and transcended. These boons are to be considered as the four directions, so that everywhere and on all sides there is auspiciousness — and protection.

5) "Meditate on the Five Seats of the Devi, all situated under My Feet."

As was earlier described, the Five Seats — Brahma, Vishnu, Rudra, Ishvara, and Sadasiva — represent the elements of earth, water, fire, air, and ether. These are their earthly correlations. But their spiritual significance corresponds to the waking (*jagrat*), dreaming (*svapna*), deep sleep (*sushupti*), transcendent (*turiya*), and beyond transcendent (*atitarupa*) states of Awareness. Thus, there is much to contemplate with this rich and variegated form of rarefied quintuplication.

6) "Perform concentrated japa and offer the results to Me, the Devi."

Arriving at the essence of the practice, here the mantra has its chance to penetrate deep into the subconscious and unconscious levels of the mind and do its purificatory work. After the previous stages of this prescribed meditation have been instigated and engaged, this phase of real practice brings forth both major shifts and hidden abilities in human awareness. These are brought about in conjunction with repetition of the mantra in formal sitting practice, not just in a general usage of the mantra during daily activities. That is, the mantra has a certain facility when utilized out in the world amidst the public, but its greatest benefit is conferred during formal meditation.

7) "Perform puja for Me with devotion, and with all sacred offerings."

Though pujas can be long and varied, a shorter description of the Mother's worship according to Her in the *Srimad Devi Bhagavatam*, is placed below:

"*Beginning with arghya, the worshiper should purify the elements and prepare the offerings, sprinkling them while reciting the Astra mantram, 'phat!' Then, closing the ten quarters with the Chotika Mudra, the worshiper should bow down to his guru. Then, taking his permission from the Devi, he should envision his external seat and purify it with his mind's thought and meditate on his inner seat (heart chakra). Then he should invoke the Devi and place Her on these two seats by steady concentration (prana prathistha) and perform the Avahana Mudra.*

"*Presenting Her with green grass, rice, and water (arghya), water for bathing Her feet (padya), water for Her bath (snaniya), some fine clothes (vastra), and all sorts of valuable ornaments, scents, flowers and other necessary articles — all with the utmost devotion — he should then also worship Her attendant deities. He can then offer Her sanctified foods and tasty dishes (naivedhya).*"

8) "Make offerings to all the deities of My sacred Mandala."

As is related above, making offerings to the attendant deities on the altar and in the shrine room is auspicious. If one cannot do this daily, the Devi says, it can be done once a week. The scriptures advise that this is best performed on Fridays.

9) "Recite My many Names and read My Upanisads."

The sacred act of scriptural study is indispensible for spiritual life. The so-called spiritual lives of many seekers are devoid of this element, rendering their power for penetrating maya and piercing the chakras ineffective. Thus, most aspirants remain on the outside of spiritual life, and many teachers do as well — all due to their underestimation, or resistance, to scriptural study. The Devi concurs, asking all votaries to complete this most important phase of Her worship. In one of Her *Upanisads*, the *Taittiriya*, it is written in this regard: *"Speak the truth. Follow prescribed conduct. Be not heedless of the solemn study and recitation of the scriptures. Never be indifferent about receiving and imparting the wisdom of the Vedas."*

10) "Dance joyfully and sing My Names."

Not to be taken as an excuse or license to engage in egoic showboating or prideful demonstration, the sincere devotee will enter into such practices in the proper spirit. The entire heart is to be offered to the Goddess, as well as the body and its movements. Then no false premises or pretenses will arise. Natural and spontaneous movement will be the result.

11) "Feed the hungry, the holy, and the devotees."

Far from being a mere act of occasional charity, such a directive from the Goddess — She who feeds all beings — is really permission to keep the mind on all beings so as to serve them at every juncture of spiritual life. This divine act of remembrance is far above the likes of an altruistic endeavor, and far beyond the realm of individual good karma. It is actually the service God in all beings. For, if one strives to serve human beings, they will tend to act like human beings. But if one serves God in living beings, they will instead tend to act Godlike. This is the secret of work as Worship, labor as Love.

12) "Perceive youth, the aged, the poor, and the public, all as forms of Me."

One of the most defining and challenging of all spiritual practices is the attempt at seeing God in everyone, in everything. This is "eyes open meditation." Instead of expecting all to flow easily, as many pseudo-devotees do, the real devotees of the Divine Mother know the real value of the relentless testing of the soul, as well as its purifying properties. The lessons around the inscrutable presence of maya are then well learned, and a return to any form of ignorance in the future will be rendered impossible. In this way weakness will get replaced by strength, indeterminate behavior by clarity and force of will. For, all of the four classes of beings listed here exhibit positive and negative qualities. Seeing the Goddess residing in them all is a teaching for the individual and for all involved.

13) *"Perform all actions in the light of the great Devi Mantra."*

As is said, even in the West, *"Thought is father to the deed."* Knowing this, the seeker of Truth brings sensitivity and higher Consciousness to bear on all acts undertaken in life. Just as a deep awareness of the meaning of food and its conscious ingestion forms an integral part of initial practice in Kundalini Yoga, so too does constant repetition of the mantra play an important role in rendering all acts pure and free of karma. Care must be taken by the aspiring seeker, however, to make sure and use the mantra in deep meditation, not just in action (as is mentioned in step three and six of this meditation and commentary). Otherwise the mind may tend towards external life only and fail to develop the ability to go within and realize the more subtle aspects of Consciousness.

14) *"Meditate on My Thousand-petalled Lotus."*

A step seldom advised by many teachers, especially until the prerequisites of spiritual practice are well attained, this final phase of meditation invites the seeker into the indiscernible realm of formlessness. There, in that spaceless space, all is an indeterminate mass of pure, conscious Awareness and Bliss. The reuniting of Kundalini Shakti with Paramasiva in this lotus is the final word in spiritual realization, equivalent to the Asamprajnata Samadhi of Patanjala, and the Nirvikalpa Samadhi of the Vedanta. As the Goddess Herself is wont to say, *"This is the greatest secret of all Gitas, so carefully contemplate it in your heart of hearts."*

≈ 7 ≈

The Devi Gita

A New Translation

In the preceding chapter the opportunity was offered to engage in a rare kind of guided meditation, using the scripture, "Devi Gita," as the source. Buried deep within one of the most voluminous scriptures of Mother India, the "Devi Gita" forms the fortieth chapter of the seventh book of the *Srimad Devi Bhagavatam* — a great work which would not be available to us in English if not for the sure and dedicated work of Swami Vijnanananda, one of Sri Ramakrishna's direct disciples.

What follows is a new English translation of this hidden gem, to be utilized for the elucidation and inspiration of the people of this more modern time. Gitas, divine songs, abound among India's rich philosophical and religious firmament. So it is meet and welcome that contemporary culture have access to the Divine Mother's own song, expressed willingly and ecstatically for the benefit of Her precious spiritual children.

To describe the golden setting in which this rare gem is placed, the Divine Mother of the Universe, known herein as the Kundalini Shakti, has descended on earth and is speaking to King Himalaya of rarefied spiritual heights, answering a host of questions put to Her by him on behalf of the gods. In one of the richest sections of this rather esoteric work, practically unknown outside of India, rarely studied even inside of India these days, The Devi speaks out Her wisdom on meditation:

The Devi Gita

Rise up, my noble child, from your deep sleep state each morning,
and meditate with loving heart and peaceful mind
on My thousand-petalled seat at the crown of the human head.
At this auspicious time think fondly and reverently of your Guru,
the epitome of graciousness, side by side with His precious Shakti
and bow down to him with offerings of heartfelt love.
After praying for his welfare, envision Me, the Highest Shakti,
the Kundalini Devi, and propitiate Me with these winsome words:

"I take complete and utter refuge in Thee, oh Devi Kundalini,
Thou inwards and upwards rising Chaitanya,
Who is Supreme Consciousness, Goddess of the Brahmarandhra,
the Shining Gateway into the Infinite Brahman —
the lofty aperture out of which the illumined soul takes flight
at that auspicious time of departing the body."

After this, My precious child, focus your awareness swiftly
on the ever-blissful Form of Mine abiding in the root chakra,
the Muladhara, as I dance amidst the Fire of Kula Kundalini there
which dwells at the very root and core of your existence.

Upon completion of this profound and heady meditation,
do thou take thy bath and perform thy duties with full awareness.
Then return to thy asana with a mind to undertake My worship,
entering divine sankalpa with sheer determination to satisfy Me.

Oh child of Mine, now take up the five great elements —
earth, water, fire, air, and akasha —
and render them exceedingly pure for My puja and worship.
Perform lovingly the sacred mudras, mantras, and nyasas
which were taught to thee by your Guru, and enter peace sublime.
Now recall, with vivid and divine memory, My Mantra,
and let it percolate within, in divine order, with all its matras.

Envision the matra "Ha" in the Muladhara chakra;
Manifest the matra "Ra" in the Anahata chakra;
Lovingly place the matra "I" in the Ajna chakra at the brow;
And bestow the matra "M" and the entire bijam "Hrim"
victoriously upon the crown of your head.
Then meditate with rapt attention on this,
My Hrillekah Mantra, with all appropriate observances.

In this pristine holy atmosphere, precious divine lover of Mine,
you must construct the Cosmic Seat of My Five Regents.
Produce this mentally in your heart chakra, My devotee,
by creating virtue, wisdom, dispassion, and prosperity
as the four stout legs of this august throne
and nonvirtue, ignorance, passion, and poverty
as the foundational body of this Universal Seat,
its four quarters pointing East, South, West, and North.

Without pause, oh ardent worshiper,
Reverently place upon this wide throne the five divine personages
— Brahma, Vishnu, Rudra, Ishvara, and Sadasiva —
who form My own divine chair,
and with heart thrown wide open by full-blown pranayam,
ecstatically meditate upon Me in that heart region, resplendent.

In this rapt and loving meditation, oh Kundalini sadhaka,
duly connect My five holy regents with the five great elements
and all these ten with the five states of your Awareness —
Waking, Dreaming, Deep Sleep, Transcendence, and Beyond —
and deftly cognize My form hovering above them all.

Meditating upon Me all set up in this rare and hidden fashion,
now enter into the holy act and atmosphere of Japam.
Lost in that deepest concentration known only to the yogis
emerge in due time and make over the fruits of your japa to Me.
Now complete your puja in traditional fashion, blissfully.

With arghya as your first offering,
prepare all other elements, sprinkling them with holy waters,
reciting with concentrated power the Astra mantram, 'Phat!'
Closing the ten quarters with the Chotika Mudra,
bow down, oh pujari, to your eternal guru within, and his Mother.

Then, taking inner permission from Me, the Devi,
envision your external seat, purifying it with your mind's thought,
and meditate on this inner foundation in the heart chakra.
Invoke My Presence there, on My throne, and on yours,
and place Me reverently on both seats by steady concentration.

Now perform the Avahana Mudra, awestruck, reciting:
"I present You, oh Devi, green grass, fine rice, and water,
with water for bathing Your feet, and water for Your bath,
with fine clothes to enhance Your incomparable beauty,
and all sorts of valuable ornaments, scents, flowers
and other necessary articles — all with the utmost devotion.

"I also worship Your five divine attendant Deities
with offerings of flowers, kum kum, and sandal paste,
and present You with sanctified foods and other tasty dishes.
And all the time, oh Devi Kundalini, I acknowledge You
as the Principal Deity, my Primordial Mother Goddess,
as Bhuvaneshvari, whose wisdom rays pervade the Three Worlds."

My Thousand Names, the Sahasranama, the Devi Suktam,
the Devi Atharva Shiro Mantra, and the Upanisads —
all My mantras — now await your recitation for My satisfaction.
Then, with the hairs of your body standing straight due to ecstacy,
and with tears of love flowing profusely from your eyes,
and with voice choked with inner feelings of love and exuberance,
dance and sing sweet devotional music to Me with a joyful heart.
For My glories are well-sung in all the Vedas and Puranas,
so for My delight, offer everything that pleases Me, daily.

And there is another selfless act that delights Me immeasurably.
After completing My homa and puja, and all other pious acts,
do thou go and feed the people with sumptuous prasadam —
the brahmins, the well-clothed young virgins,
the handsome youths, the public, and especially the poor —
worship them all devoutly as so many forms of Me.

With all this well accomplished, then bow down before Me,
the Supreme Deity dwelling within your heart and mind.
Then offer up the Samhara Mudra to attain closure,
and take leave of the worshiper's ritualistic form and seat.
Remember, especially at this time, My Great Hrillekah Mantra,
the chief of all mantras; all actions should be accomplished with it.

I am always reflected in this clear mirror of My Hrillekah Mantra,
so never forget it; all mantras are rendered fruitful if offered in it.
It is conferred upon you by the Guru, My special Emissary.
Always revere that One and consider yourself blessed by his grace.

Oh Father of the Great Snow Mountains, oh Himavan!
Confirm within that nothing remains unavailable, at any time,
to the one who worships Me, the Kundalini Devi, sincerely.
After quitting this body, that one receives a rare boon —
entrance into My own special abode, difficult of attainment,
known as Mani Dvipa to the saints, sages, and seers,
the Jewel Island of Mother Essence.
There, such a fortunate soul gets the very form of the Devi,
and the devas and other beings always bow in deference to him.

Oh Mahidhara, both holder and summit of Bhur Loka:
I have described to you the rules for worshiping the Great Devi.
Consider all of this well and worship Me as to your qualifications.
Then you will attain your goal; of this there is no doubt.

Remember, too, oh best of high-born souls,
This fine shastra, the Devi Gita; it is not to be given out lightly.
Do not offer it to those who are not devotees,
to those who are enemies of the dharma,
or to those who are clever and cunning.
To give it out hastily in such a fashion
is like stripping the cloth off of the breast of a mother.

This Great Song of Mine ought to be given to a worthy disciple,
a burgeoning bhakta, a noble son or daughter,
to those who are good-natured and blessed with intelligence.
At the time of departing or celebrating of the ancestors,
this song ought to be read out loud for the common good of all.
Thus is My Word, to be held sacred, and be cherished by you.

With this divine telling of the fortuitous appearance of the Devi
before the stunned and delighted form of King Himalaya,
and Her discourse on how to invoke and worship the Most-High,
the Holy of Holies among all existing Deities, The Divine Mother,
the Great Lord, Maharishi Vedavyasa,
closed the Seventh Book of His profound Mother Scripture,
The Srimad Devi Bhagavatam, of 18,000 nectar-filled verses.

Om Peace, Peace Peace!

Harih Om Tat Sat!

Appendix

Further Significance of Food

The involved and often complex subject of food is of great importance to people, even beyond the need for human survival. And this fact holds true of spiritual aspirants as well who, when they approach the religious preceptor for clarification of scriptural matters, methods for the destruction of delusions and misconceptions, and instructions on meditation, invariably form questions around food and its role in spiritual life. This appendix, expanding on page eleven of the first chapter of this book, is meant to address both relative and subtle topics and issues concerning food and its role in spiritual life thereby inspecting the facets of bodily health, vital functionings, mental refinement, and intellectual expansion.

Food in India's Past

In the Upanisads, in one of its seven foundational Peace Chants, it is written: "*May our bodies experience great health; may our lifeforce flow unimpeded; may our minds expand in their capacity to know Brahman.*" This bold, many-faceted expression shows without a doubt that the ancient rishis of the Vedic period in India were the earliest of wholistic practitioners, concerned with all levels of existence but focused ultimately, in the interim of life and living, upon realization of the formless Reality. When one thinks along these lines, august names such as Lord Vasishtha and Lord Patanjali come to mind, whose specific but interconnected philosophies included mindfulness of all levels of the marvelous human being's delicate system.

As an inspection of India's history is made, as much as we know of it and can glean, it becomes obvious that fealty and worship of God with form was a special part of it. Divine aspects such as Vasundhara and Annapurna, what to speak of Lakshmi and Ganesh, epitomized the copious flow of foodstuffs in cornucopia-type fashion to the multitudes. And unlike many other cultures, the concept of food was extended to include sustenance (Vishnu) for the mind and intellect as well; nourishment was not left at the physical level only.

And in fact, since both asceticism and monasticism, what to speak of Yoga, were practiced by many, the idea of moderation, even renunciation, became both familiar and desirable to seeking souls. The ability to do without was thereby developed overall, which added both practical and spiritual dimensions to the culture.

On the latter side, it was noticed that an excess of food taken into the system slowed it down and made the mind sluggish, whereas minimal ingestion not only kept the vessel trim, but also saved it wear and tear and maintained it in a fit condition. What is more, it was observed that going without food entirely for a short period of time actually sharpened the senses, and clarified the mind and its thinking process. The will portion of the mind complex (antahkarana, the fourfold combination of dual mind, thoughts, intellect, and ego) then came to the fore and exercised its prerogative for higher life — spiritual life. For, whereas many beings often think of entering into religious life, most never get around to it due to the overshadowing of the will by the dual mind and the ego. In brief, without spiritual life, there is no true life at all.

Types and Qualities of Food

In the beginning of spiritual practice the aspirant is not yet free from the physical effects of ingesting food. The will is weak. Refraining from foods which are tamasic and rajasic figures in here. The chart on the facing page addresses this:

The Four Clarities of Spiritual Life

Chart by Babaji Bob Kindler
Property of SRV Associations

3 Qualities of Food

1. Tamas
"Is stale, tasteless, over-cooked, impure — refuse."

2. Rajas
"Is bitter, sour, saline, hot, pungent, and dry."

3. Sattva
"Gives vitality, energy, vigor, health, and joy."

(Sri Krishna, Bhagavad Gita)

5 Defects of Food

1. Poor soil, lack of nutrients
2. Selfish purpose while harvesting
3. Lack of awareness when processing
4. Impure mood while preparing
5. Failure to bless and consecrate

1. Annaprasada (Clarity of Food)

The 5 Aids for Steadiness of Mind

1. Enthusiasm
2. Courage
3. Steadfastness
4. Pursuit of Wisdom
5. Serving the Great

(utsaha, sahasa, dhairya, adhyatma-vidya, and mahat-seva)

The 4 Causes of Distraction

1. Sorrow
2. Despair
3. Unsteadiness
4. Uneven breathing

(duhkha, daurmanasya, angamejayatva, and shvasaprashvasah)

2. Chittaprasada (Clarity of Mind)

The 4 Beneficial Attitudes

1. Friendship
2. Mercy
3. Positivity
4. Indifference

(maitri, karuna, mudita, and upekshanam)

The 4 Deadly Traps

1. Grief
2. Guilt
3. Depression
4. Lack of Self-worth

(shoka, udvega, vishada, and vibhranti)

3. Samprasada (Clarity of Mood)

The 3 Conditions of True Detachment

1. Spiritual Attainment
2. Free of Afflictions
3. No Transmigration

(sampadana, klesha- & samsara-vinashana)

The 3 Obstacles to True Detachment

1. 8 Occult Powers
2. Heavenly Existence
3. Personal Lordship

(asta-siddhis, vaikarika-bandha, & prakrti-laya)

4. Adhyatma-prasada (Clarity of Spirit)

A dharmic teaching for life in India revolves around the word "prasad." Basically, it means clarity, but has come to be considered as synonomous with sanctified food almost exclusively. The chart on page 87 shows the four areas of human life where clarity is most needed. For our purposes here we look to the first category at the top of the chart, Annaprasad, to find the teaching around the qualities of food.

We find there that tamasic food is impure, overcooked, old and lifeless. It is easily and obviously avoided by most beings. Only those who are devoid of mindfulness and basic awareness would consider its intake into the body. Rajasic food, according to Sri Krishna, is that which assaults the senses, which causes upheaval to both the senses and, later, to the stomach and digestive system. Only sattvic food is advised, and only those who have refined their sensibilities will adhere to it. It brings vitality, meaning the emergence of health-promoting prana, mukhyaprana.

What to Eat, What not to Eat, How to Eat, and Why

But a more important teaching appears in the next column — that of the five defects in food. This teaching applies to those who have transcended rules for food, having already put them in place or, due to circumstances, being unable to have access to the kind of food that they would otherwise prefer to ingest. In other words, all food is subject to defects prior to the time of ingesting, even so-called sattvic foods. Lack of nutrients in the soil and scarcity of water during the growing season, the selfish or lackadaisical mind set of those who harvest the foodstuffs, the base and greedy thoughts of those who process the food for market and for sale, and the impure mind and thoughts of those, including ourself, who prepare the food for consumption — these four defects, in various combinations, pervade food.

Fifth, and as stated in this book as a key element to proper and traditional Kundalini Yoga practice, is the failure to bless the food with higher mind and intellect. Just as there must be mental asana, not just physical asana; just as there must be informed pranayama rather than mere observance of breath, so too must there be conscious and intelligent sanctification of our food rather than a mere grateful acknowledgement of its presence.

A subject of interest in this regard is the search by contemporary spiritual practitioners for what is called "organic" food. The idea is to avoid foods which have been sprayed with insecticides — a wise move in a world which values money and cosmetic appearance over natural processes and wholistic health. With this as a given for most informed souls, the fact of the matter turns out to be that our so-called wholism in modern times is missing many of its own necessary facets. First, it caters to the body only, overlooking — either out of ignorance or complacency — the need for feeding the vital, mental, psychological, intellectual, and especially the philosophical and spiritual levels of our being. Secondly, it has not looked into the five defects in food, all of them intrinsic to its very nature, and adjusted accordingly.

And there is a third and connected reason why eating naturally, organically, and "wholistically," often misses the point entirely. Mankind should not merely live to eat, but must eat to live. True life is what is at stake here. As the Kundalini Yoga system demands of its practitioners, when the food has been blessed consciously with words of purificatory power, the seeker must wait, with awareness, for the infusion of energy from sanctified food and consciously take it upwards, inwards, refining it for usage in spiritual endeavors. This sublimation process leads to true life, dharmic life — not a life of mere pleasure and happiness attended by suffering and sorrow.

And even if the aspirant possesses only an active nature, is not yet imbued with knowledge, devotion, or the power of inward contemplation, he/she can still use this refined energy, called Ojas, for service of God in mankind. Many have done so; many are doing so. It is evident, then, at least to philosophical systems and their founders, what the early secrets to true life consist of, and what the current oversights of modern day people consist of. As for what the remaining secrets consist of, the reader is encouraged to study the other three clarities on the chart on page 87 for clues and teachings — clarity of mind, clarity of mood, and clarity of Spirit.

Sexuality and Food

Another topic which should be addressed, and which involves a connection with the subject of food, is human sexuality. The sublimation of energy herein described and advised by Kundalini Yoga involves the close and careful monitoring of the sexual impulse of human beings, its control, and sometimes its outright cessation. Persons considering and entering into monastic ways of life and similar institutions are required to practice celibacy (brahmacharya), thereby both becoming aware of the presence of sexual power and learning to utilize it to aid in the quest for spiritual realization. Others, called "householders" in Indian dharma, also observe periods of celibacy, and practice moderation of the sexual urge. By such cycles of abstinence all may learn to regulate this powerful force and bring it "up the spine" for higher uses. Interestingly enough, and among other valued qualities, the power of retentive memory is aided by celibacy and moderation, as well as the maintenance of a healthy body and aware mind late into life.

As to the dynamics of combining consecrated food with sublimated sexual energy, in the same way that mantra acts upon food to render it pure, in that same way does sanctified food conduce to a purer form of sexual energy — one that is not frenetic, driving, lustful, and therefore uncontrollable. Then, like food that is considered pure and sacred, the sexual act will also come to be considered such — the consecrated and loving union between the masculine and feminine aspects of the Divine.

Food and Samskaras — Connections to Past Lifetimes

The camel eats thorny bushes, despite bleeding gums, yet it nevertheless goes on ingesting them due to that peculiar taste that it loves. This prime example, humorous and sobering at the same time, was utilized by Sri Ramakrishna to indicate the presence of samskaras (mental impressions in the subconscious and unconscious mind) leading to rebirth.

In all living things, and inclusive of spiritually undeveloped human beings, they seek what they are most accustomed to according to their desires. This stark and unforgiving rule rides with death and thereby reaches into future existences. Just as a camel departs its worn out form and, due to its desire to ingest certain types of foods, searches for parents which will provide such material for its next lifetime as a camel, so too will a human being do the same. If a human soul, stunted and darksome, becomes addicted to drugs in its previous life or lives, and goes to death in this lamentable condition, it will thereafter search for parents who are in a similar plight so as to have access to addictive substances. No one can blame God for this; neither God nor devil can receive the responsibility. It is all due to one's own samskaras. If one finds that "there is the devil to pay," then take it up with the devil called the ego self. And freedom from such maladies? That too is up to one's self.

To put it simply, like attracts like. Samskaras are impressions in the mindstuff (thoughts) which dictate the future movement of the soul in relativity. Positive and negative both, and based upon past actions, they formulate the temperament and character of any given human being through a series of lifetimes. Genetics, heredity, and the like are only the effects of these — samskaras. This is both a hard fact and a great key. That is, recognition, or lack thererof, of the presence and influence of karma (action), its effects (samskaras), and reincarnation can either make or break the human being's direction and potential arrival into lower and higher worlds (the chakras/lokas).

A study of samskaras will benefit all levels of existence. Most important will be the application of the science of samskara and its wise reading to the raising of children, for an advance awareness of where the soul has been previous to the present embodiment and its advantages and drawbacks can be gleaned by spiritually aware parents, allowing them to make much more informed decisions as to the child's future. For instance, even such things as the type of food (physical, mental, intellectual, etc.) a child prefers will confer an inkling of the quality of consciousness present there. A natural desire for sattvic ingestion — nutritious foods, mental acumen, and intellectual pursuits and interests — can be recognized and cultivated early on, before the negative samskaras can kick in and bring up all manner of impediments leading to potential ruination.

The possibilities are endless. But first, western cultures must learn to look to the East, especially to India, and begin to apply this esoteric knowledge to their science, psychology, medicine, philosophy, and life in general so that subtle knowledge of this nature can come to the surface and be utilized. The end result will be a realization that, as the Vedanta affirms, "All is Food," as in ancient times, and this will usher in an age of pervasive wisdom scarcely seen since that more enlightened period of the Indian rishis, many millennia ago.

Sanskrit Glossary

Achaman — Purification of the palate represented by the rinsing of the mouth, wherein water is taken to cleanse it prior to repeating sacred mantras and slokas in ceremonial worship.

Acharyas — Great teachers, usually appearing as the leaders in charge of entire lineages.

Adhara — In Kundalini philosophy, a subtle chakra in the muladhara region which contains Kundalini Shakti, i.e., "adhara," container; in Vedanta, the name for the five sheaths of the Adhara system which encircle Atman, or Consciousness.

Adhyatma-vidya — Science of the Self, Atman.

Advaitic — Referring to Advaita, the nondualistic philosophy of the Vedanta.

Advaitists — Those who follow Advaita philosophy.

Adyashakti — The original Shakti, self-willed, all-intelligent.

Agama — Scriptures in general, mostly referring to the Tantras.

Agni — The deity of fire.

Ahamkara — Ego, not so much as a personality or an attitude, but as a principle which causes the sense of separation of the embodied soul from formless Awareness.

Ahimsa — Nonviolence; one of the five yamas of yoga.

Aim — The bijam for Sarasvati indicative of growth and learning.

Ajna chakra — The sixth spiritual center, sometimes called the "Third Eye," associated physically with the space between the eye brows but aligned specifically with Taparloka.

Akhanda Satchitananda — Absolute Reality which is indivisible.

Akartrtvama — The quality and practice of moderation.

Akritih — Referring to one's essential nature.

Akasha — Space, atmosphere, of which there are five — Bhutakasha (space of objects); Pranakasha (space of lifeforce or vital energy); Chittakasha (space of mentation); Jnanakasha (space of intelligence); Chidakasha (space of Consciousness).

Alinga — Of the category of the formless, or an "unmarked" principle in Yoga.

Anahata chakra — The fourth chakra, correlated physically with the heart region, but specifically aligned with Maharloka.

Ananda — Absolute and unalloyed, uninterrupted, Bliss.

Ananda Ghana — Mass of Bliss, meaning Brahman, the Absolute.

Ananda Sagara — Ocean of Bliss.

Angamejayatva — The problem of weak, unsteady or uncomfortable limbs, which is a distraction to Yogic equipoise.

Angas — Limbs, as in Ashtanga, the eight limbs of traditional Yoga.

Anugraha — Grace.

Arghya — Purification of the five elements to be used in sacred ceremony (puja).

Asamprajnata — Seedless Samadhi in Yoga, meaning formless, correlative with the Nirvikalpa of Vedanta.

Asanas — Postures or positions conducive for meditation, which in Kundalini Yoga are mental stances first, and physical thereafter.

Asta-siddhis — Referred to as well as the Astabala-siddhis, they are the eight occult powers which deter the aspirant from full realization.

Astra Mantra — A mantra that raises powerful defenses and supplies weapons against various ailments, impediments, and enemies.

Asteyam — Nonstealing, which is one of the five yamas of Yoga.

Astika — Full faith in the truth of the scriptures.

Atharva — One of the four Vedas, the youngest, used primarily by the ancient Indian priests called "atharvas," which contains many chants, hymns, invocations and incantations in connection with marriage, birth, death, illness and other areas of life.

Atala — One of the hell realms, or lower realms of existence.

Atitarupa — Beyond formlessness.

Atma Vichara — In-depth introspection of the nature of the true Self of human beings.

AUM — The sacred syllable of Brahman.

Avahana — A mudra or sacred hand position used in special worship ceremonies.

Avatars — Divine Incarnations, of which there is but one who takes various forms from age to age.

Avinashantam — Indestructible and peaceful nature of Reality.

Avyaya — That which is changeless and inexhaustible; a particular yoga of the Divine Mother path.

Banalingam — A subtle atmosphere in the Anahata, or heart chakra, where Siva dwells.

Bhadrasana — A beneficial body position.

Bhagavad Gita — The sacred wisdom song of Sri Krishna, which is one of the three most hallowed scriptures in Indian religious tradition.

Bhakta — An adherent of the path of devotion, or Bhakti Yoga.

Bhavamukha — A state of samadhi wherein the luminary perceives both the world and nondual Reality simultaneously.

Bhava Samadhi — A state of ecstasy filled with intense bhakti.

Bhur — The first word of the holy Gayatri mantra, signifying the physical worlds and all objects and beings therein.

Bhurloka — The realm of physical objects, and the first of seven inward-reaching levels of consciousness, and the plane of physical beings — humans, animals, insects, and plants — corresponding to the Muladhara chakra.

Bhuvarloka — The realm of heaven proper, the third of seven inward-reaching levels of Consciousness, corresponding to the Svadhisthana chakra, wherein reside the ancestors, celestials, siddhas, and munis.

Bhuvaneshvari — A beloved form of the Divine Mother of the Universe, who is Goddess of the Earth.

Bhuvar — The second word of the holy Gayatri mantra, signifying the ethereal and subtle worlds and all beings residing therein.

Bijam — Literally, "seed," having to do with the root syllable of power in the mantra, like Aum and Hrim.

Bindu — In the Tantras, a concentrated point from whence all manifestation flows forth.

Bodhisattvas — Beings who take vows of loyalty which bring them to earth for a series of lifetimes in order to help others reach the enlightened state.

Brahma — The Lord of Creation who projects the worlds at the time of new beginnings or cosmic cycles.

Brahmacharya — Celibacy; one of the five yamas of Yoga.

Brahmagranthi — In Kundalini Yoga, a formidable block, like a subtle membrane, found in the first two chakras, and which must be pierced in order that the soul transcend rebirth in ignorance.

Brahmaloka — The seventh and highest of the seven inward-reaching realms of Consciousness (which correspond with the seven chakras). Consciousness here is scarcely in a "state," or "center," or "realm," but is closest to Its pristine condition as formless Awareness.

Brahmanadi — The covering to the opening of the Sushumna which, when pierced, allows for Kundalini Shakti to course inward and flood the seven centers with spiritual power.

Brahmarandhra — The gateway to the seventh chakra which leads from the Third Eye center to the thousand-petaled lotus at the crown of the head.

Brahmins — The priest class.

Buddhi — Higher Intelligence, to be distinguished from the mental buddhi as the intellectual sheath which contains intelligence.

Chaitanya — Pure, conscious Awareness, which is Supreme Reality in Indian religion and philosophy.

Chakras — Spiritual centers, or vortexes, which receive and conduct Kundalini Shakti.

Chakshu — Eye; to see.

Charya — A spiritual preceptor; qualification.

Charya Pada — One of the four great undertakings of Siva in Tantra.

Chid — Pure, conscious Awareness.

Chetana Samadhi — A samadhi of the mind and intelligence which allows for remembrance of the depth of experience even after it has passed.

Chitta — "Stuff of the mind," meaning its thoughts, concepts, content, projections, imaginings, etc.

Chotika — A powerful mudra used in puja and sacred ceremony to bring certain aspects of the worship to a close.

Danam — Charity; generosity.

Darshanas — Paths of clear seeing, referring to the Six Orthodox Darshanas of India — Sankhya, Nyaya, Vaisheshika, Yoga, Purva Mimamsa, and Uttara Mimamsa (Vedanta).

Daurmanasya — Despair; one of the four causes of distraction in Yoga practice.

Daya — Compassion.

Devas — The gods, or "shining ones," inhabiting realms higher and subtler than that of the ancestors and celestials.

Devi Mahatmyam — Also called the Chandi, it is one of two or three essential Divine Mother scriptures of India.

Dhairya — Boldness; courage.

Dharana — Concentration, which is the sixth of the eight limbs of traditional Yoga (Patanjala); a particular yoga of the Divine Mother path.

Dharma — Divine Life, lived in accordance and observation of the precepts, laws, and axioms of dharma.

Dharmic — Having to do with the dharma and its influence.

Dhyana — Meditation proper, which is the seventh of eight limbs of traditional Yoga.

Diksha — Initiation, also called *mantra-diksha*, through which the aspirant is ushered into the path of spirituality and its practice and aims.

Dhrti — Patience, specifically of a spiritual nature.

Duhkha — Pain; sorrow.

Eka — The Sanskrit word for the number "1."

Ekasana — One asana, meaning that the ultimate aim of Yoga is to settle into one bodily position — the one that affords the longest and deepest practice of meditation.

Ekananda Chidakrtiih — An exquisite name of the Divine Mother of the Universe — indivisible, aware, blissful, and ever-content.

Ganesha — The elephant-headed god with one tusk who, when evoked and propitiated, confers benefit, protection, and auspiciousness on all undertakings of life.

Gaunamukti — Liberation, but of a slow and indirect kind.

Gitas — Songs of spirituality, of which there are many in Indian religion and philosophy.

Granthi — Knot, referring to a barrier or impediment which hampers spiritual progress.

Granthis — Knots in the physical, emotional, pranic, mental, psychological, intellectual, philosophical, and even spiritual levels of the human psycho/physical being.

Gunas — The three gunas of *tamas, rajas,* and *sattva* which correspond to the principles of lassitude, restlessness, and balance in the human mind. All three, even balance (sattva), are to be transcended, as their presence signals the disequilibrium which ushers in the worlds of name and form in time and space.

Guru — Spiritual preceptor, whose grace and aid are indispensible.

Guru Tattva — The principle of teacher found in all beings, all things.

Harih — As in *Harih Om Tat Sat,* a profound utterance on intrinsic oneness with God, Hari, Brahman.

Hatha — A school of Yoga focused on body postures and breathing exercises, whose original purpose was to strengthen the body and purify the nervous system so as to help make them fit for spiritual life and meditation. In later centuries, and especially in present times, the system's aims have degraded into the search for bodily health, occult powers, and longevity. As Svatmarama states in his *Hatha Yoga Pradipika* (16th century), *"Raja Yoga begins where Hatha Yoga leaves off."*

Himalaya — The famed king of the eternal snow mountains to whom the Divine Mother, Uma, was born.

Himavan — Referring to King Himalaya.

Hiranyagarbha — The Cosmic Egg, or Golden Egg, often perceived as one or similar with the Cosmic Mind or Mahat, Unmanifested Prakriti, and even AUM. Anthropomorphically it corresponds directly with Lord Brahma of the Hindu Trinity.

Homa — The sacred fire ceremony utilized in Vedic rites and rituals, and into which various articles are offered which signify the purification of an aspirant's thoughts, words, and deeds.

Hri — Modesty.

Hrillekah — The most powerful bija mantra of the Divine Mother path which, when added to one's sadhana and recited devoutly, brings full spiritual realization to the ardent practitioner.

Hrim — The specific bijam of the Hrillekah mantra.

Iccha — Divine Will, referring to the Iccha Shakti, one of three or four aspects of Divine Mother Reality, the others being Jnana Shakti, Kriya Shakti, and Dravya Shakti.

Ida — The subtle left-hand channel/nadi and its current running along the spine, opposite the Pingala and next to the Sushumna.

Ishtam — The Chosen Ideal upon whom the devotee meditates in the shrine of the heart, realizing an ineffable presence in deepest contemplation.

Ishvara — Same as Ishtam, and referring to the Divine Personality of God with form; one of the five seats of the Devi.

Ishvara Pujanam — The worship of God with form.

Jada Samadhi — A stunned state of consciousness caused by powerful internal visions of various types.

Jagrat — The first of four states of a human being's awareness, that of waking consciousness; see also svapna and sushupti.

Janaloka — The realm of the great spiritual beings, the fifth of seven inward-reaching levels of Consciousness, corresponding with the fifth chakra, the Vishuddha.

Japa — The practice of recitation of the mantra given to the disciple by the illumined preceptor at the time of initiation into the spiritual path.

Jiva — the embodied soul.

Jivanmuktas — Those liberated beings, having gotten freedom while in the body, who then embody and reflect the highest state of Awareness for other beings.

Jivatman — The Atman existing in the form of the embodied soul, but as yet unrealized.

Jnana — Wisdom, specifically of the spiritual type.

Jnana Chakshu — Another name for the Third Eye; sixth chakra.

Jnana Shakti — One of the four main aspects of the Mahashakti.

Jnana Pada — One of the four main works undertaken by Siva.

Jnanendriyas — The five organs of knowledge, i.e., hearing, touching, seeing, tasting, and smelling.

Jnanis — Knowers of the highest wisdom pertinent to the revealed scriptures.

Jyoti — Light, specifically of the intelligent and spiritual kind.

Kala — Time; a name for Siva.

Kaivalya — Isolation; in Yoga, the penultimate aim of separation of the Soul from nature.

Kapila — The revered systematizer of the Sankhya philosophy.

Karana — Cause; the name of the third body of the nonself of man, the other two being gross and subtle — Sthula and Sukshma.

Karmendriyas — The five organs of action, i.e., speaking, acting, locomotion, procreation, and excretion.

Karuna — Compassion.

Katha Upanisad — The Upanisad which tells the story of Nachiketas and his visit with Yama, the Lord of death.

Klesha — An impediment in Yoga, like egoism and ignorance.

Klim — A sacred bijam for regeneration and transformation.

Krim — A sacred bijam for insight and perfection.

Kriya — The name of one of the four main aspects of Shakti, along with Iccha, Jnana, and Dravya Shaktis, whose workings are spontaneous and lightning swift; one of the four main works, padas, of Lord Siva, which deals with divine and dharmic activities.

Kriya Pada — One of the four main works undertaken by Siva.

Ksa — What is enduring, eternal; the name of one of the petals of the Ajna Chakra.

Kshama — Forgiveness.

Kula — Pertaining to family, as in Siva's family; as in Kula Kundalini, the power that exists in the purificatory fire within the Muladhara Chakra.

Kumbhaka — The sustained portion of the breathing process; the samadhi that occurs when the breath becomes naturally suspended in an adept or master.

Kundalini — Literally, "coiled up," referring to the spiritual potential in mankind that lies dormant in the Muladhara Chakra.

Kurukshetra — The battlefield upon which Sri Krishna transmitted the wisdom of Vedanta to Arjuna during the war between the Pandava and Kaurava clans.

Lakshmi — The Goddess of abundance and beauty.

Lamas — Tibetan holy men, usually monks, who represent the Buddha dharma via the Tibetan tradition.

Linga — The root syllable of Lord Siva called "sva," which dwells in the Svadhisthana Chakra; in Yoga, a designation of all that is "marked" with form, as opposed to what is alinga, "unmarked" or formless.

Loka — A realm of existence that, unlike the physical planets in outer space, exists within, and which are gradated into various levels which host ancestral, celestial, subtle, and causal beings.

Lokas — A collection of internal realms.

Mahadeva — A name for Lord Siva, meaning "Great God."

Mahamaya — Literally, "Supreme Maya"; a powerful name for the Divine Mother of the Universe which points to Her as the overseeress of all of Existence.

Maharloka — The fourth of the internal realms of Existence that corresponds with the Anahata Chakra of the Kundalini system.

Mahashakti — Literally, "Great Shakti," which is a name for the Divine Mother of the Universe as the pervading intelligent power in all things, all beings.

Mahat — Referring to the Great Mind, or God's Mind, which in the Sankhya Yoga system is the causal hub of all that is formless, and which later gets projected into form.

Mahatala — One of the seven lower worlds or hell realms.

Mahat-seva — Service of the holy ones.

Mahavidya — Literally, "Great Wisdom," signifying the Mother of all Wisdom who fashions worlds out of living intelligence.

Mahendranath Gupta — The author/compiler of the epic spiritual testament titled the *Gospel of Sri Ramakrishna*.

Mahidhara — A name for King Himalaya, who is the foundation and overseer of the earth realm.

Maitri — Friendliness.

Mandala — Sacred diagram representing a region, sphere, or plane of existence.

Mangalam — Auspiciousness.

Manana — Rolling the meaning of slokas and teachings over and over in the mind; one of the three proofs of Truth.

Mani Dvipa — A unique and special world where the Divine Mother of the Universe presides, and where souls who take Her as their Chosen Ideal repair to after passing from the body.

Manipura chakra — The third chakra, associated in physical terms with the region of the stomach but specifically aligned inwardly with the realm of Svarloka, or heaven.

Mantras — A collection of Sanskrit word formulas that aid the Vedic priest in performing worship and help the spiritual aspirant purify, refine, and clarify the mind, preparing it for samadhi.

Mantri Guru — That singular and exemplary spiritual teacher who initiates the sincere aspirant into spiritual life and its practice.

Matra — Unit; a letter which comprises a portion of a sacred word, such as AUM, in which the A, U, and M are each matras.

Maya — The worlds of name and form in time and space based in causation.

Maya shakti — A name for the Divine Mother.

Mayic — Of, about, or referring to anything that is of the realm of name and form in time and space, based in causation — Maya.

Mudita — Joy.

Mudra — Any of a series of significant hand positions used to sanctify such articles as food, the five elements, flowers offerings, and certain rites and rituals of Vedic worship.

Mukhyaprana — The essential constituent in the five forms of prana which, when flowing, conduces to perfect health in the body. This health, gotten from taking sanctified food with a reverential attitude, is a sign that the mukhyaprana is ready to be refined via spiritual disciplines and transformed into Ojas.

Mukti — Liberation, or the state of freedom always at hand.

Mula — Root.

Muladhara Chakra — The first and primal chakra, associated physically with the base of the spine, but specifically aligned with the Bhurloka holding human beings, animals, insects, and plants.

Nadi — A subtle nerve that conducts pranic energy and, when purified, acts to carry spiritual vibrations as well.

Nadis — The overall network of thousands of subtle nerves running through the human body/mind mechanism.

Naivedhya — Sanctified food offering for the deities.

Nididhyasana — Realization of the Truth in meditation, gained after hearing and analyzing it.

Nirvana — State of total absorption into Reality, like Nirvikalpa.

Nirvichara Samadhi — Samadhi free of mental vibrations and thought-forms.

Nirvikalpa — Literally, "beyond all thought forms" including time, equating to the deepest formless samadhi, nondual in essence.

Nirvitarka Samadhi — Samadhi free of intellectualization.

Niskala — Partless, spotless.

Niyamas — The five preliminary spiritual observances — purity, contentedness, study of scriptures, austerity, and devotion to God — practiced by the aspirant of classic Yoga prior to sitting (asana) and breathing exercises (pranayama); also, the ten niyamas of Tantra.

Nyasas — Renunciation; a collection of practices performed in ritualistic worship which divest the pujari of conventional assumptions and mental overlays.

Ojas — The spiritual power which culminates as a result of commingling the ingestion of sanctified food with recitation of mantra, heightened vital energy, and spiritual disciplines.

Om — Same as AUM, the most sacred bijam or seed syllable, which is seen as the Word of Brahman sporting a myriad of connotations and blessings.

Omkara — Om, or AUM, as the cause of all manifestation.

Pada — Feet; a word used to designate the four works of Lord Siva on earth (or His four footsteps), namely Jnana pada, Yoga pada, Charya pada, and Kriya pada.

Padma — Lotus, indicating the seven chakras of the Kundalini system.

Padmasana — A physical posture conducive to meditation.

Padya — Water offering, which is one of the sixteen elements of Vedic ceremonial ritual.

Panchamahabhutas — The five elements.

Param — Supreme.

Paramahamsa — "Great Swan," a name for a unique type of illumined soul who is simultaneously a superlative teacher and a past master of spirituality.

Paramasiva — The ultimate nature of Lord Siva, His supreme aspect as formlessness.

Paramatman — The supreme Soul, unique in comparison to its lesser manifestations such as the Jivatman.

Paravidya — Higher knowledge, spiritual wisdom of revealed scripture and direct spiritual experience, as contrasted to ordinary (dualistic) scripture and intellectual knowledge (aparavidya).

Parigraha — Giving or receiving in abundance; the names of Lord Siva's two main shakti forces which oversee the projection and sustenance of the worlds.

Patalas — Literally, "sunken grounds," referring to the hell realms, seven in number, corresponding with the seven lokas and seven chakras, namely Atala, Vitala, Sutala, Talatala, Mahatala, Rasatala, and Patala.

Patanjala — The classic name of the Yoga darshana of eight limbs, which bears its systematizer's name.

Patanjali — The founder, father, or systematizer of the classic Yoga of Patanjala.

Pingala — One of the two nadis or main subtle nerves which surround the Sushumna, the other being the Ida.

Pitham — Seat or basis.

Pradhana — The name in Sankhya Yoga which designates the existence of unmanifested Prakriti, or Nature in its formless state before quintuplication and solidification.

Prakriti — Nature, both manifest and unmanifested, which is insentient as opposed to Purusha, the Sentient Self or Soul.

Prakriti Karma Kriyamanani — The state of mind which knows that all action takes place in nature, not in the Soul.

Prakriti-laya — The state of those who stop short of full realization to involve themselves in manipulating subtle nature and its potential.

Pranava — Another designation for Om, signifying it as the origin of prana in all its forms.

Pranayama — Specialized breathing exercises in Yogic practice which help the aspirant recognize the pervasive nature of prana and bring it under control for the purpose of purification of mind and Self-realization.

Pranic — About or having to do with prana.

Prasad — Sanctified food, which is served to the devotees following ritualistic worship and blessing.

Prasadam — Same as prasad.

Pratistha — Steady, firm.

Pujari — Qualified person who presides over Vedic worship or puja.

Puja — Ceremonial worship wherein offerings and devotions are rendered to the deities.

Puraka — The inbreath, which is one of the three or four phases of the breathing process.

Purnahanta — I in Fullness.

Puranas — Secondary scriptures of India, as contrasted to the primary scriptures such as the Upanisads and Bhagavad Gita.

Raja Yoga — Another name for Patanjala, or Ashtanga Yoga.

Rajas — One of the three gunas, or modes of nature, signifying energy in nature and restlessness in the mind.

Ramakrishna — A spiritual luminary of 19th century Bengal who is considered by many to be the Avatar of the Kali yuga.

Ramprasad — A celebrated Bengali poet/saint of India.

Rasatala — One of the lower worlds or hell realms.

Rechaka — The outbreath, which is one of three of four phases of the breathing process.

Rishis — Illumined souls of the Vedic period in India who were seers of the Truth, and whose descendants distilled the ancient wisdom into sacred texts like the Upanisads.

Rodhini — An extremely subtle minor chakra which lies between the Ajna and Sahasrara chakras.

Rudra — Another name for Lord Siva, usually in a wrathful form.

Rudragranthi — In Kundalini Yoga, a block, like a subtle membrane, found in the fifth and sixth chakras, which must be pierced in order that Kundalini Shakti reach the Sahasrara chakra.

Sadasiva — The highest and eternal form of Lord Siva, very generous and very blissful; one of the five seats of the Devi.

Sadhana — Specialized spiritual exercises and disciplines which qualify the sincere aspirant for awakening to the presence of the chakras in the gross, subtle, and causal bodies, all leading to realization of nondual Truth and samadhi.

Sadhaka — A seeker of spirituality; one who engages in sadhana, spiritual discipline.

Sagarbha — A type of mantra practice wherein the mantra is chanted in conjunction with visualization of the Ishtam, or form of God.

Sahasa — Courage.

Sahasranama — The thousand names, meaning any of a host of such lists that are chanted in propitiation of various deities.

Sahasrara chakra — The seventh chakra, often not designated a chakra at all, associated in physical terms with the crown at the top of the head but specifically aligned inwardly with the realm of Brahmaloka and beyond, i.e., nonduality.

Sakala — Literally, "with time," or attended upon by time.

Samadhi — Any of a host of rare spiritual experiences, usually of the wisdom variety but not exclusive of devotional bhavas and moods, wherein the practitioner beholds levels of inner consciousness leading up and into the nondual state.

Samatva — Steadiness on the spiritual path.

Samhara — A mudra used to bring to a close a puja or section of a puja; destruction/dissolution.

Sampadana — The boon of spiritual attainment in sadhana.

Samprajnata Samadhi — All the samadhis of Yoga that fall within the realm of form; seeded samadhis.

Samsara-vinashana — The destruction, or seeing beyond, of the idea of relativity.

Samskaras — An important word in Sanskrit and Indian philosophy referring to impressions left in the mind by repetitive past actions that, in the case of negative impressions, and when left unneutralized, cause the transmigrating soul (mind complex) to return to rebirth again and again.

Sanaka — A great and celebrated rishi of Vedic times who was the mindborn son of Lord Brahma and counselor to Lord Vishnu.

Sananda Samadhi — The samadhi of Yoga which is still attended by individual bliss, i.e., not yet formless or nondual.

Sanatkumar — One of the four sons of Lord Brahma, and the oldest progenitor of mankind.

Sanchita karma — Karma of the past, created by actions in previous births and taken up in successive lifetimes for neutralization.

Sankalpa — The vibrational activity of the mind complex which sets in motion worlds in space and time, all projected at the cosmic, collective, and individual levels in conjunction with one another.

Sannyasins — A class of high-souled individuals who have renounced conventional life and possessions and who live freely, spending their time and energy teaching humanity how to do the same.

Saptarishis — The seven original rishis of India who respectively preside over the seven worlds or lokas: Bhurloka, Bhuvarloka, Svarloka, Maharloka, Janaloka, Taparloka, and Brahmaloka. The names of these great ones change as the ages do, but the ancient Vedas have them listed as Gotama, Bharadvaja, Vishvamitra, Jamadagni, Vasishtha, Kashyapa, and Atri.

Sarasvati — The name of the Vedic Goddess, also called the Goddess of the Wisdom Word, who presides over the spiritual arts and sciences as well.

Sarvatra Samavathistam — The state of mind which perceives God dwelling in all things equally.

Sasmita Samadhi — The samadhi of Yoga which is still attended by the sense of ego, therefore not yet formless or nondual.

Satsanga — A gathering of beings who seek Truth first and foremost, and who search for answers to issues and concerns inhibiting Its manifestation and expression.

Sattva — One of the three gunas of nature, signifying balance in nature and happiness in the mind.

Satyam — Truthfulness; one of the five yamas of Yoga.

Saucha — Purity; one of the five niyamas of Yoga.

Savichara Samadhi — A samadhi of Yoga which is attended by reasoning and deliberation.

Savikalpa Samadhi — Conditioned Samadhi of Vedanta, as contrasted to Nirvikalpa which is unconditioned.

Savitarka Samadhi — A samadhi of Yoga which is accompanied by intellectual rationalization.

Shabda — Another designation for Aum.

Shakta — A follower of the Divine Mother and Her pathways.

Shaktayika — The intensely living power of Awareness of the Divine Mother of the Universe.

Shakti — Dynamic spiritual energy.

Shaktis — Any of a host of powers emanating off of the Divine Mother of the Universe, the main four of which are Iccha (will), Jnana (wisdom), Kriya (spontaneous action), and Dravya (creativity).

Shaktiman — The wielder of shakti power.

Shankara — The great Advaitin whose scriptures and commentaries figure as one of the highest authorities in Vedanta philosophy.

Shankaracharya — Same as Shankara, with the addition "acharya" designating him as a great teacher.

Shiro Mantra — A powerful mantra amongst a collection of great mantras of the Divine Mother.

Shiva — Same as Siva.

Shraddha — Faith.

Shravana — Hearing the Truth, which is the first of the three Proofs of Truth.

Shruti — Scripture of the most authoritative kind, superior to Smriti and Itihasa; to be heard.

Shvasaprashvasah — Uneven breathing, which is one of the four distractions in Yoga.

Siddhantavakya — Words which are the final conclusion on a subject.

Siva — The Lord of Wisdom, and third of the Hindu Trinity of primary Deities; one of the five seats of the Devi.

Sivarupa — The very form of Siva.

Slokas — Statements that make up a scripture.

Spandas — Internal vibrational fields of awareness, like realms or lokas.

Sri Sarada Devi — The revered and blessed wife and spiritual consort of Sri Ramakrishna Paramahamsa, believed by thousands of living beings to be the Incarnation of the Divine Mother in this age. She was confirmed by Sri Ramakrishna to be an incarnation of the Goddesses Kali, Lakshmi, and Sarasvati conjoined.

Sristhi — Creation, in Indian philosophy and religion meaning the projection of worlds via the vibrations of Mind in its cosmic, collective, and individual aspects.

Srimad Devi Bhagavatam — One of a few quintessential Mother scriptures of India and the most authoritative text of the Shakti tradition.

Sthita Samadhi — A state of steady samadhi.

Sthiti — Steadiness.

Sthula — Gross, meaning apparent, not subtle; one of the three bodies of mankind, namely gross, subtle, and causal.

Sukshma — Subtle; one of the three bodies of mankind, namely gross, subtle, and causal (sthula, sukshma, and karana).

Suktam — Beautifully and well-recited; a collection of verses chanted to various deities.

Sushumna — The "central channel" along which are arranged the seven chakras of Kundalini, and around which circle the Ida and Pingala nadis.

Sushupti — Deep sleep state, often correlated with formlessness, and the "M" of Aum; see also jagrat and svapna.

Sutala — One of the lower worlds or hell realms.

Svadhisthana chakra — The second chakra, associated in physical terms with the region of the sexual organs, but specifically aligned inwardly with the realm of Bhuvarloka.

Svadhyaya — Study, recitation, and memorization of scripture as a prerequisite to other spiritual practices like asana and pranayam, and pratyahara. It is one of the ten yamas and niyamas of traditional Yoga (Patanjala).

Svaha — A designation for the third loka, or Svarloka, it is also a pronouncement of auspiciousness used in ceremonial worship.

Svapna — The dream state, or second of mankind's three states of consciousness (waking, dreaming, and deep sleep), associated with the "U" of Aum; see also jagrat and sushupti.

Svarloka — The realm of higher heavens, and the third of seven inward-reaching levels of consciousness which sport gods and goddesses and those beings who gather around them — corresponding to the Manipura chakra.

Svastikasana — A physical posture helpful in meditation.

Svatantriya — Freedom, or state of absolute Independence of the spiritual kind.

Svetashvatara — The name of one of the more recent Upanisads, containing teachings of powerful merit and boundless scope.

Swami — The title given to monks of the Hindu religion who have taken monastic vows and received authority to teach spirituality to others.

Taittiriya — The name of one of the major Upanisads containing many slokas about spiritual life and living, including the sanctification of food.

Talatala — One of the lower worlds or hell realms.

Tamas — One of the three gunas, or modes of nature, signifying inertia in nature and slothfulness in the mind; see also sattva and rajas.

Tanmatra — The rudimentary state of matter before the quintuplication process of the five elements takes place.

Tantras — Literally, "that which saves," they are a collection of scriptures that, along with the Upanisads, Bhagavad Gita, Brahma-sutras, and others, make up the Sanatana Dharma, the eternal religion of India.

Tantric — Having to do with the Tantras, and specifically the worship of deities such as Vishnu, Siva, and Divine Mother.

Taparloka — The realm of seers and luminaries, the sixth of seven inward-reaching levels of consciousness, corresponding with the sixth chakra, the Ajna.

Tapasya — Rigorous spiritual disciplines, called austerities; one of the five niyamas of Yoga.

Tat — "That," in reference to Brahman or Reality.

Tattva — A wisdom principle that, when meditated upon with the purified mind and intellect, releases profound insight contributing to the attainment of Samadhi.

Tattvas — Relating to the Twenty-four Cosmic Principles listed in the Sankhya Philosophy of Lord Kapila that profoundly influenced all of India's major darshanas such as Buddhism, Yoga, and Vedanta.

Tejas — The light of refined Awareness used by illumined souls to teach and transmit spirituality to others, and which can even be seen emanating off the personages of great souls.

Tirodhana — Self-limitation; in the Shakta view, Lord Siva, the Mahashakti, and their projections appearing under the limitation of form due to inherent will.

Turiya — Literally, "The Fourth," referring to the fourth state of Awareness beyond waking, dreaming, and deep sleep. It is synonymous with the highest Samadhi, i.e., Asamprajnata in Yoga and Nirvikalpa in Vedanta.

Tushti — Contentment; satisfaction.

Udghata — A force of spiritual awakening that is a precursor to the actual rising of Kundalini Shakti. It is an intrinsic testing mechanism which naturally measures whether the aspirant is ready and prepared for higher spiritual states, i.e., rising to the higher chakras.

Udvega — Guilt, one of the four deadly traps in Vedanta.

Uma — An august name for the Divine Mother of the Universe, consort of Siva.

Unmana Samadhi — A state of samadhi which takes one beyond the mind.

Upanisad — The distillation of Vedic Wisdom, specifically around nondualism or Advaita. The word has been defined as "the proximity to the spiritual luminary which loosens the knot of ignorance and ushers in freedom."

Upanisads — A collection of 108 still existing scriptures of Mother India, considered as primary scriptures which must be heard.

Upasana — The spiritual science which emphasizes worship of and meditation on the deities, or God in His/Her multifarious forms.

Upekshanam — Equanimity of mind.

Urdhvaretoyogi — That yogi or yogini in whom the spiritual force is rising up the spine, or moving inwards. Such beings practice the sublimation of energy gotten from food that is blessed by mantra and subjected to the fire of Yoga via intense spiritual practices.

Utsaha — Enthusiasm.

Vaikarika bandha — Bondage to heavenly existence.

Vairagyam — Detachment, or dispassion, which forms one of the four key practices of Vedanta. In it the sadhaka first masters discrimination between what is real and what is unreal, and then detaches from the latter.

Vajrasana — A physical posture which is conducive to meditation.

Vak — Word, referring to those power-laden words which make up the scriptures and the guru's discourses containing wisdom transmission.

Vayu — The god of wind/air, but referring here to the "spiritual wind," or Mahavayu, which courses through the human mind/intelligence complex and leads the meditator to higher states of Awareness.

Vedas — The four cardinal scriptures of the ancient Indians, of the

Vedic period, out of which the later Upanisads developed. The Upanisads form the fourth section of the Vedas, the first three consisting of rites and rituals, hymns and devotional songs, and rules for those who retire to the forest after earthly life is fulfilled to practice spiritual disciplines.

Vedavyasa — Looked upon as "the Father of Vedanta," he collected many of the ancient scriptures of India upon the turning of an age, and thereby saved them from possible extinction.

Vibhranti — Poor estimation of oneself; lack of self-worth.

Vicchinavastha — Vasanas as hidden desires, which are harbored in the subconscious mind, and which will fructify later.

Vichikirsha — Divine Desire, sometimes called the "demiurge," to project the worlds of name and form, from the highest right on out to the atomic.

Videhamukti — Liberation of the disembodied kind, wherein the soul enters into the formless state, seldom to return.

Vigarbha — A type of mantra practice wherein the mantra is chanted in conjunction with the sacred syllable Aum, leading to meditation on the formless God.

Vijnananandaji — The monastic name of one of the sixteen direct disciples of Sri Ramakrishna, he is credited, among other things, with translating the Srimad Devi Bhagavatam into English, thus helping spread its profuse Mother Wisdom to the West.

Vindusthan — Another name for the Sahasrara Chakra.

Virasana — a physical posture which is conducive to meditation.

Vishada — Depression.

Vishnu — The Lord of Sustenance who, along with Brahma and Siva, form the divine Trinity of India.

Vishnugranthi — In Kundalini Yoga, a block, like a subtle membrane, found in the third and fourth chakras, which must be pierced in order that Kundalini Shakti ascend to the Vishuddha and Ajna chakras.

Vishuddha Chakra — The fifth chakra, associated in physical terms with the region of the throat, but specifically aligned inwardly with the realm of Janaloka.

Vitala — One of the lower worlds or hell realms.

Viveka — Discrimination, or discernment, which forms the first of four great practices in Vedanta (Sadhanachatushtaya) by which the aspirant learns to separate the essential from the nonessential. Its acquisition signals the beginning of true spiritual life and real attainment.

Vivekachudamani — The profound scripture by Shankara, perhaps his most well-known which transmits many of the foremost teachings of Vedanta in its 580 nectar-like slokas.

Yamas — Five preliminary practices in Yoga – nonviolence, truthfulness, nonstealing, continence, and nonreceiving of gifts – which form the basis for early spiritual discipline in traditional Yoga, i.e., ahimsa, satyam, asteya, brahmacharya, and aparigraha; also, the ten yamas of Tantric practice.

Yantra — A mystical diagram, talisman, or spiritual apparatus used in Tantric rites that, when utilized by adepts, bring benefit to life and spiritual endeavor.

Yoga — The overall practice of spirituality, which is also the goal of embodied beings seeking to realize Truth and Self.

Yoga Pada — One of the four main works undertaken by Lord Siva.

Yogas — Referring to the four main yogas, namely, Raja, Jnana, Bhakti, and Karma, but inclusive of a host of others, such as Kundalini Yoga.

Yoginis — Women practitioners and adepts of the Yoga darshana.

Yuga — One of four ages or extended phases of time that, when placed together end on end, make up what is termed a Mahayuga — individually called Satya Yuga, Treta Yuga, Dvapara Yuga, and Kali Yuga in order of manifestation.

CPSIA information can be obtained
at www.ICGtesting.com
Printed in the USA
LVOW13s0058130217
524076LV00030B/1411/P